AF593325

They Call it Courage

By the same author

Flashing Blades
Brabham, Story of a Racing Team
The Classic Mercedes-Benz
Like Father, Like Son
Rally of the Forests
The Book of the Veteran Car
The Car Makers
Great Disasters
Inns and Harbours of North Norfolk

They Call it Courage

The Story of the Segrave Trophy

PHIL DRACKETT

ROBERT HALE · LONDON

First published in Great Britain 1990

Robert Hale Limited
Clerkenwell House
Clerkenwell Green
London EC1R 0HT

British Library Cataloguing in Publication Data

Drackett, Phil, *1922–*
They call it courage : the story of the Segrave Trophy.
1. Sports. Trophies, history
I. Title
796.079

ISBN 0–7090–4028–8

Photoset in Sabon by
Derek Doyle & Associates, Mold, Clwyd.
Printed in Great Britain by
St Edmundsbury Press, Bury St Edmunds, Suffolk.
Bound by WBC Bookbinders Limited.

Contents

To 'Brecky',
Fifth Marquess Camden
– a true and loyal friend

Illustrations

PICTURE CREDITS

Castrol: 1–2, 18, 27, 31–2, 35, 38. Ford Motor Company: 3–4, 11–12, 29–30. Lejeaune: 5. *Autocar*: 7. RAC: 10, 17, 33, 37. Sport & General: 13. *Flight*: 14–15. Hawker Aircraft: 16. Associated Press: 21. Fred Taylor: 25. Goodyear: 28. Lady Camden: 39. Citroën: 40. Keystone Press: 41

JACKET CREDITS

Front, colour: Ford. *Front, b/w:* Barratts. *Back, colour:* Ken Wallis

Preface

Small boys are hero-worshippers. My first hero was Open Golf Champion Harry Vardon who bent to shake a five-year-old by the hand with all the respect of an equal. Then there was Bob John, Arsenal and Wales half-back, another friend of my father and as cultured a gentleman off the field as he was a player on; 'Nella' Tarleton, a boxing champion of supreme skills, who took the trouble to write to a small boy with advice on how to box; and Jack Dunfee, one of the famed 'Bentley Boys' (who five times drove the giant Bentleys to victory in the Le Mans 24-Hour Race) whom many years later I was to interview when he was one of London's leading theatrical impresarios.

Yet of them all, Sir Henry O'Neal De Hane Segrave, racing-driver and record-breaker, held first place in the affections of my younger brother and myself.

Although I was but seven at the time, the morning of 14 June 1930 when my father, a copy of the *Daily Express* in his hand, opened my bedroom door and quietly said, 'Sir Henry Segrave's dead,' has remained in my memory. Not only small boys mourned that day, a nation mourned ...

Segrave had been 'the most courageous man I ever met', according to Lord Wakefield, the oil tycoon who had supported many brave men in their record-breaking attempts.

A trust fund was set up to perpetuate Segrave's memory and a trophy awarded, usually annually, to other brave men – and brave women – who would follow in his footsteps in upholding British prestige before the world.

Little did I know that day in 1930 that one day I would

find myself Secretary of the Segrave Trophy Awarding Committee, something which makes me wonder how much things are ordained in this world of ours.

In the following pages I have tried to do justice to the story of Segrave; to the trophy; and to the courageous people who have earned it.

PD
Mundesley-on-Sea
August, 1989

Acknowledgements

My thanks are due to Harry Calton, Public Affairs Manager of the Ford Motor Company, without whose help and encouragement this book would not have been written. Thanks also to Steve Clark, Head of Ford's Photographic Services, for his help with illustrations. Most of the photographs used are from Ford, the RAC, Castrol and Dunlop, but whatever the source we have tried to credit it where possible. In some cases, however, we have been unable to trace the source and we can only ask the photographers concerned to accept our thanks.

Thanks are also due to G. G. Bayes, son of the man who sculpted the Segrave Trophy; Louise Irvine, Director Historical Promotions, Royal Doulton, and an authority on the work of Gilbert Bayes; Derek Guy and his successor at Castrol, Richard Price; the RAC; and my old friend, Pat Gregory.

Rosemary, Lady Camden, has given me her full support and I am also very grateful to many of the past winners of the trophy and my fellow-members of the Committee for their recollections and their help. Last but by no means least my thanks to Derek Barron, Chairman and Chief Executive of the Ford Motor Company and Chairman of the Segrave Awarding Committee.

Part I
Segrave's Legacy

1 *The End – and the Beginning*

The sleek white hull of the motor-boat scudded across the dark waters of Lake Windermere, gathering speed with every second, its three occupants mere specks to the hundreds of watchers, some in other boats, many more on the shore.

Suddenly the motor-boat snaked, the bow raised from the water and the crew were thrown out. When rescue craft reached the scene, the motor-boat, *Miss England II*, was floating upside-down; one engineer, Vic Halliwell, was dead with a broken neck; the other, Michael Wilcocks, thankfully alive. And the pilot, Britain's greatest racing-driver, Sir Henry Segrave, was also alive – just. Despite both arms and two ribs being broken, a thigh badly crushed and injuries to his head, he was still conscious.

A launch ferried him to Belle Grange, a house on the western shore of the lake and Lady Segrave, who had been watching from the Lancashire shore, was taken to him there. He asked her if he had regained the world water speed record for Great Britain. She said he had. Two-and-a-half hours after being taken from the water, he died from haemorrhage due to a perforated lung. He was thirty-three.

Until that fateful moment on Windermere, Segrave had borne a somewhat charmed life. Born in Baltimore, USA, son of an English father and an American mother, who died when he was a baby, he was educated at Eton, leaving that establishment to join the Army when the Great War commenced in 1914.

Gazetted a Second-Lieutenant in the Royal Warwickshire Regiment, he arrived in France in January 1915. Infantry subalterns were short-lived in those horrifying days. They led their men out of the trenches and across No Man's Land and were usually the first to be picked off by the enemy riflemen. Segrave lived through the slaughter of Neuve-Chapelle and the hell which was the Second Battle of Ypres but was twice wounded, first through the wrist and then more seriously through the left shoulder and chest, which was what the troops called 'a Blighty one' because it was serious enough for the man concerned to be sent back to 'Blighty', otherwise England, to recuperate.

While on sick leave, Segrave developed a burning ambition to fly and on his return to active duty he applied for a transfer to the infant Royal Flying Corps, predecessor of today's Royal Air Force.

Flying a DH2, a single-seater De Havilland pusher (the propeller was behind the pilot instead of in front) biplane, armed with one machine gun, he shot down an Aviatik C11 two-seater artillery observation plane on 16 May 1916, but five weeks later was himself shot down by an LVG, escaping with nothing worse than a shaking.

Shortly afterwards, flying one of the new FE8 scouts, he was brought down by anti-aircraft fire. Again he survived but this time he was not so lucky and suffered a badly broken left ankle. To enable him to walk again, silver plates were inserted in his foot, an impediment which makes his subsequent career on land and water and in the air all the more remarkable.

Around this time he met an attractive musical comedy actress, Doris Stocker; they fell in love and were soon married. Now promoted to major, he was sent to the United States, land of his birth, as a member of an aviation commission whose task was to assist the development of military aviation and training. Doris went with him.

Introduced to motor-racing at the Sheepshead Bay track on Long Island, he lapped an Apperson at 82 m.p.h. and was now bitten by the speed bug. On his return to the United Kingdom he tried to get a place in the STD (Sunbeam-Talbot-Darracq) team but, perhaps not surprisingly since his experience was limited to a few circuits of Sheepshead Bay, he was politely turned down.

Undeterred, he bought a 1914 Grand Prix Opel and

entered it at Brooklands but in his very first race a wheel flew off at more than 100 m.p.h. Exhibiting tremendous coolness and skill, Segrave held the car steady and came safely to a halt.

Forty-five minutes later, in what was only his second race and using the same car, he registered his first victory. Two more wins, three seconds and three thirds followed before the 1920 season ended and in 1921 he got his wish, a place in the STD team.

It was hardly a vote of overwhelming confidence. He was to drive the team's *fourth* car, meet his own expenses and pay for any damage to the car. Imagine the reaction of your modern Grand Prix driver if offered such a deal.

As a try-out, Segrave drove a Grand Prix Sunbeam at the Brooklands Easter Meeting and won with ease. Determined to make the most of what he saw as his big chance, he went into strict training and gave up smoking and drinking, at least temporarily.

The French Grand Prix that year was run over a very rough circuit and was a menace to tyres. Segrave had to change his no less than fourteen times and for good measure his mechanic was knocked out by a flying stone, the oil tank was holed by another and the engine developed trouble all on its own. Segrave finished ninth and last of the survivors but he had finished and that earned him a regular place in the team, an occasion he soon celebrated by winning his first big event, the 200 Miles Race at Brooklands.

During the years that Segrave raced at Brooklands a small boy was taken there to see him. The lad was a distant relative and what he saw at the Weybridge track was to make him a lifelong motor-racing aficionado.

That small boy grew up to be an announcer and commentator at Brands Hatch and Silverstone, on the Brighton Run and, because he was multilingual, at Monte Carlo and other famous international circuits. He also ran an East End boys' club which was supported by Graham Hill and many other motor-racing aces. His name is Anthony Marsh and although I've known him many years it was only recently that I learned that it was Segrave who, in Anthony's words, 'started me off'.

In 1922 Segrave broke the lap record in the Tourist Trophy race and was second in the Coppa Florio. His reputation was growing and in 1923 he won 'the big one', the French Grand Prix, then regarded as the world's top motor race. When Segrave's Sunbeam took the chequered flag it marked the first time in history that a Grand Prix had been won by a British driver in a British car. That year he also won the Boulogne Grand Prix, a race for light cars, or voiturettes as they were known in those days.

Magneto trouble robbed him of a second successive victory in the French Grand Prix of 1924 but there was consolation when he won the Spanish Grand Prix on roads made treacherous with rain and splattered with sticky clay.

The Spaniards called him 'El Maestro Completo' in admiration of the way the cool, calm Englishman coped with the extraordinary conditions.

Although Segrave continued racing and scored more wins – the 200 Miles Race at Brooklands in both 1925 and 1926, the Grand Prix de Provence in the same years and the famed Shelsley Walsh Hill-climb among them – it would not be until 1960 that a British driver in a British car would win another major Grand Prix.

Between the wars, the only British drivers to win major Grands Prix apart from Segrave would be William Grover and Dick Seaman and neither won in British cars. Grover drove for Bugatti under the pseudonym 'Williams' and most people believed him to be French. He was an Allied agent in the Second World War and was executed by the Nazis. Seaman, one of the best-ever British drivers, drove for the German Mercedes works team. He was killed in a racing accident before the war began.

During 1926 Segrave made an attempt on the World Land Speed Record. Sunbeams had built a V-12 4-litre car especially for the task and it had been designed by Louis Coatalen. Nevertheless, the car proved something of a disappointment and there were a great many 'bugs' in the engine which had to be sorted out.

Southport Sands had been chosen as the venue for the attempts and Segrave 'enjoyed' some bumpy rides before he broke the existing record at a speed of 152.33 m.p.h.

The final record run was hair-raising and at one point the car hurtled through the air after running into a patch of extra-soft sand.

Despite this the venture had given Segrave a thirst for more record-breaking and in 1927 he decided to retire from motor-racing in order to concentrate on records. He was probably the greatest driver of his time, having won 31 races in 49 starts and undoubtedly further success would have come his way had he not been diverted by the battle to be the fastest man on land.

Meanwhile, first Parry Thomas and then Malcolm Campbell had beaten Segrave's record, the latter setting a target of 174.88 m.p.h.

Far from disheartened at their earlier, barely successful attempt, the Sunbeam company were building a new contender, a car powered by two giant 400 hp Matabele aero engines. The aim was to be the first past 200 m.p.h. Segrave – De Hane as he was known to most of his friends (his full name was Henry O'Neal De Hane Segrave) – estimated that he required a level stretch of some ten miles in which to work up speed, hit the measured mile and then slow down again at the other end. Daytona Beach in the United States fitted the bill.

This decision brought the Americans into the international fold. Previously records set in the United States had not been recognized elsewhere but Segrave changed all that.

He set sail for the States in the *Berengaria* but while he was still on the ocean there came bad news. Parry Thomas, making another attempt on the record at Pendine Sands, had been killed.

Segrave might easily have shared the gallant Thomas's fate. At the end of his first run, the Sunbeam's brakes failed and the car ran into the sea. Fortunately it swerved landwards and he turned around to run over the measured mile again, climbing out of his cockpit to hear from the timekeepers that he had clocked 203.79 m.p.h. – the first man in the world to travel at more than 200 m.p.h. He was a national hero.

No one could take the honour of being first to the magic 200 away from Segrave but the record itself was not to last for long. First Campbell edged past it by a modest 3 m.p.h.

and then the American Ray Keech, in a brute of a car, the three-engined *White Special*, raised it higher. Frank Lockhart, who like Keech had made his name on America's most famous race-track, the Indianapolis 'brickyard', was also in the lists in a beautiful car, small by record-breaking standards, the 3-litre *Stutz Special*. His bid was to end in his death. They wanted Keech to make the record safe for the States but the Indy pilot had had enough of the hard-to-handle monster, the *White Special*, and he flatly refused to drive it again. A lesser-known driver, Lee Bible, volunteered to take over but Keech knew best, Bible being killed in a vain attempt on the record.

So Segrave came into the picture again. Major Irving had designed for Sunbeam what was arguably the most attractive land-speed-record car ever built. The *Golden Arrow* lived up to its name, representing the apogee of streamlining not only at that time but for a long time to come. Painted gold from end to end, it looked very much like an arrow and, more importantly, went like an arrow, powered as it was with a Napier engine similar to those used in the famous Schneider Trophy seaplanes.

On the sands of Daytona, the *Golden Arrow* waltzed away with the record, clocking up a figure of 231 m.p.h. The car never ran again but thousands of replicas were sold in Britain's toyshops and were treasured by hordes of small boys.

A large-scale model, somewhat battered, was found in the cellars of the RAC early in the 1970s and restored to its former glory to feature in the Club's 75th Anniversary Exhibition. The car itself has, it is hoped, come to its last resting place in the National Motor Museum at Beaulieu.

From that museum it was announced in 1989 that an agreement had been signed with the Golden Apple Trust to restore the *Golden Arrow* to running order.

The founder of the Trust is another man to whom British prestige and record-breaking are important. He is Robert Horne, former chairman of the national men's wear chain, Horne Brothers and a record-breaker in his own right as holder of the UK Flying Mile Record for wheel-driven cars (as distinct from pure jets).

Segrave was not a man to rest on his laurels and ten days after breaking the land speed record he was on the water in his speedboat, *Miss England*, and at Biscayne, Miami, he won the Fischer Cup Race, defeating *Miss America*, driven by the American ace, Gar Wood, in the process.

Segrave had his dander up and was determined to end the United States' domination of motor-boat racing over which Gar Wood and his countrymen had held sway for years. The Fischer Cup was followed by the Volpi Cup, the German Championship and the European Championship. Next would come the World Water Speed Record.

Yet, busy as he was, this gifted and remarkable man still found time to design a motor-car, the Hillman Segrave, and co-design a monoplane, the Segrave Meteor.

Gar Wood had dominated the water-speed scene for a decade. He had good fast boats and he was a skilled and tough competitor. He held the Water Speed Record at 92.86 m.p.h. and although he and Segrave were friends, De Hane was determined to wrest the crown from him.

Miss England II was especially constructed for the job. She cost £25,000, a tremendous sum of money then, and was powered by two Rolls-Royce aero engines, giving over 3,000 hp.

Shortly after 1 p.m. on Friday, 13 June 1930, *Miss England II* was towed out through a mass of small boats to the open water of Lake Windermere. As they boarded the craft, the engineer Michael Wilcocks had joked, 'Don't worry, Friday the 13th has always been my lucky day.'

De Hane opened up the throttles and the boat almost disappeared from the sight of onlookers in a spume of spray. They were travelling very fast as they reached the start line and roared through the measured mile at well over 92 m.p.h., turning to make the return run necessary if a record was to be claimed. Flat out, the boat came speeding back and everyone jumped for joy as the timekeepers recorded a mean speed of 98.76 m.p.h. The World Water Speed Record belonged to Great Britain.

Then came something which puzzled the watchers, one of whom was Lord Brecknock, later the Marquess Camden, and 'Brecky' to his friends. He had been to school with Segrave, worked with him at the Sunbeam Motor Company and often acted as team manager. Now he was out on the lake in charge of one of the stand-by boats.

'I was overjoyed,' Brecky was to say later. 'I realized that de Hane had broken the record and I turned my craft towards the jetty, looking forward to congratulating my old friend and joining in the celebrations.

'Then, to my surprise, I saw *Miss England* come about and speed off northwards again, travelling flat out. Then it reared into the air, pitched over and sank in a flurry of smoke and steam.

'Afterwards it transpired that de Hane had wanted to see if he could reach 120 m.p.h. Unofficially, people who had a watch on him, clocked him at just a fraction under that figure.'

Truth is invariably stranger than fiction. The only member of the crew to survive was Wilcocks, the man who said that Friday the 13th was his lucky day. Which in a way it was ...

The irony of the tragedy was that Lady Segrave who had helped and encouraged her husband in his motor-racing career – he had after all not taken up the sport until after their marriage – had grown increasingly worried about the dangers of car racing and had been somewhat relieved when he turned to motor-boats which she thought were safer. Prophetically, Segrave had told her, 'Don't worry, I shall never die in a car.'

There was considerable speculation as to the cause of the accident and the popular theory was that the propeller had sheared. This had happened a couple of times during trials. But until the boat could be retrieved from the depths it was all guesswork.

It took two weeks to wrest the boat from 190 ft of water and then, to the chagrin of the tap-room 'experts', it was discovered that the propeller was sound.

However, the step in the bottom of the boat on which the craft would plane at speed was badly damaged. Water had poured into the hole and acted like a powerful brake, violently applied, and it was this that caused the boat to rear up and overturn.

What caused the damage? Majority opinion was for a

waterlogged tree floating in the water just under the surface and indeed a piece of timber fitting this specification was recovered from the lake near the scene of the disaster.

There was one final irony. If Segrave had not decided to retire from motor-racing he would have been sharing the wheel of the victorious Bentley at Le Mans with Sir Henry 'Tim' Birkin, instead of meeting a date with destiny on Windermere.

The hero's ashes were taken up in a Segrave Meteor by his father, Charles, and scattered over the playing fields of Eton.

Just a few weeks before, his son had said, 'God save me from dying between the sheets.'

It is perhaps difficult nowadays to comprehend the impact that Segrave's death had upon the nation. There was no television and the deeds of those men and women of action who accomplished great things were brought to public attention by newspapers more concerned with good reporting than digging up or inventing scandals about people in the public eye. Consequently a very special niche was carved for many of these heroes in the hearts of the populace.

So it was with Segrave. The powers-that-be in motoring, aviation and water sport, newspaper publishers and Segrave's friends – men like Lord Brabazon, Lord Howe, Lord Wakefield, Lord Brecknock – and Lord Sempill, who had but recently introduced Segrave and other friends to the new sport of speedway racing – got together and, with the consent of Lady Segrave, raised a trust fund to administer a trophy in his memory.

Of this group, Sir Charles Cheers Wakefield, raised to the peerage as Baron Wakefield of Hythe in 1930 and the first leader of the motor industry to receive this distinction, was the man most closely connected with record-breaking.

As the man who introduced Castrol Oil to the world he backed many land-, sea- and air-record attempts between the wars, and British drivers and pilots, in particular, owe him much.

Segrave himself, Malcolm Campbell, George Eyston, Bert Hinkler, Jean Batten and the Mollisons were all aided by Wakefield.

It was fitting that, many years later, the Castrol Company would become even more closely involved in the award of the Segrave Trophy.

In contrast to his great interest in speed, Wakefield, a man of strong religious beliefs, spent much of his leisure time in social work, principally with orphanages, he and his wife, Sarah, having no children of their own.

The task of creating a trophy worthy to bear the name Segrave was entrusted to a leading sculptor, Gilbert Bayes. The result was a masterpiece of its kind, not surprising since Louise Irvine, an authority on his work, says,

> Gilbert Bayes was one of the most remarkable and versatile of British twentieth-century sculptors yet he is curiously little known today. Some of his works are universally familiar, for example, the clock above the main entrance to Selfridges; the frieze on the Saville Theatre, Shaftesbury Avenue; and Lord's Cricket Ground; but there is little popular understanding of his work as a whole.
>
> Bayes worked in a great variety of materials and media and carried out many public and private commissions in a career that spanned the Arts and Crafts Movement, the Edwardian era, Art Deco and Modernism. In his time Bayes enjoyed a considerable reputation and his career was both long and distinguished. He was a regular exhibitor at the Royal Academy and other institutions from 1888, when he was sixteen until his death in 1953 and he collected many gold and silver medals, prizes, scholarships and other awards.
>
> For many years President of the Royal Society of British Sculptors, he was also Master of the Art Works Guild. He worked in wood, plaster, ivory, bronze and other metals, stone, cement and ceramic and his output ranged from commemorative medals to large-scale public commissions in England and abroad.
>
> Above all, Bayes was a London sculptor. His studio was in St. John's Wood and there are at least eleven important works by Bayes to be seen in the streets of London.
>
> Further examples are on view in other parts of Britain, in Switzerland, Australia, France and India. There is now considerable interest in British sculpture of the twentieth century. Recent exhibitions have featured the work of some of Bayes' colleagues and contemporaries, for example, Sir Alfred Gilbert, W. Goscombe John, Frank Dobson and C. S. Jagger

> while other contemporaries, Epstein, Eric Gill and Moore are already well-known. Prices in the art market have also reflected this trend. In April, 1985, a bronze by Bayes was sold for £58,000 by Sotheby's, a price putting him firmly in the forefront of British sculptors.

This then was the man commissioned by the Segrave Trustees to produce the Segrave Trophy, plaque and medal, and posterity has endorsed the fine manner in which he carried out his task.

(Incidentally, it *is* an incredibly small world. In researching a recent book of mine, *Flashing Blades*, which is concerned with the history of ice hockey, I was able to gather information on women's ice hockey from a former captain of the England team. Her name? Jean Bayes, daughter of the sculptor and still living in the St John's Wood area.)

The Terms of Award for the trophy were drawn up as follows:

1. The Trophy shall be called 'The Segrave Trophy'.
2. The Trophy and the subscribed funds shall be vested in three Trustees, namely, the Chairman of the Royal Automobile Club, the Chairman of the Royal Aero Club, and the President of the Marine Motoring Association. The Trustees shall administer the invested funds, and shall be responsible for the fulfilment of these Conditions of Award.
3. An Awarding Committee shall be appointed, consisting of a Representative of each of the following Bodies: Institution of Automobile Engineers, Institution of Mechanical Engineers, Royal Automobile Club, Royal Aero Club, Royal Aeronautical Society, Marine Motoring Association and the Newspaper Proprietors Association.
4. The Awarding Committee shall meet in January of each year for the purpose of making the award. The Award of the Committee shall be final and without appeal, and the Committee shall have the power to withhold the Trophy if, in their opinion, there has been no performance of sufficient merit during the previous year to justify the Award.
5. The Trophy shall be awarded to the British subject who, in the judgment of the Awarding Committee, accomplishes the most outstanding demonstration of the

possibilities of transport by land, air or water. In coming to their decision the Committee shall be guided by the following paragraph extracted from the original Memorandum announcing the institution of the Trophy:

> The simple idea behind this tribute to Sir Henry Segrave is to stimulate others also to uphold British prestige before the world by demonstrating how the display of courage, initiative and skill – the Spirit of Adventure itself – can assist progress in mechanical development.

In awarding the Trophy consideration shall also be given to the extent to which the apparatus used represents in design, workmanship and material a product of the British Empire.

6. A replica in miniature shall be given to each winner of the Trophy and be his property. At the discretion of the Committee not more than Six Medals, to be retained by the recipients, may be awarded to those who were associated with the winner of the Trophy in the Performance which gained the Trophy.
7. The Trophy shall normally remain in the custody of the Royal Automobile Club and shall be insured by the Trustees against all risks while in the custody of the said Club. The winner however, shall be permitted, with the Trustee's assent, to remove the Trophy from the Club to his own possession, but he shall first satisfy the Trustees that he has insured the Trophy against all risks and made provision for the immediate return of the Trophy to the Royal Automobile Club on request by the Trustees or in the event of his death or bankruptcy. Further, the Trustees shall have the right to require the return of the Trophy to the Royal Automobile Club at any time without assigning a reason.
8. The use of the male pronoun shall mean either sex.
9. All costs and charges relating to the administration and insurance of the Trophy by the Trustees and the purchase of Replicas and Medals shall be paid out of the funds at the disposal of the Trustees.
10. These Conditions shall be binding on all concerned, but the Trustees reserve to themselves the right to withdraw these Conditions at any time, and to impose such conditions as they in their sole discretion shall think fit.

ROYAL AUTOMOBILE CLUB LONDON SW1
December, 1930

Not surprisingly, the years have enforced some changes in those conditions although the main purpose has remained unaltered. Of the three original trustees, the chairman of the Royal Automobile Club remains. The chairman of the Powerboat Division of the Royal Yachting Association has replaced the chairman of the Marine Motoring Association and the chairman of the British Aircraft Owners and Pilots Association has replaced the chairman of the Royal Aero Club.

The bodies represented on the awarding committee are much the same although the Newspaper Proprietors have become the Newspaper Publishers and the Guild of Motoring Writers has been co-opted. The present sponsors, the Ford Motor Company, are also represented on the committee and the chairman and chief executive of that company, Derek Barron, is chairman of the committee at the time of writing.

Sponsors? Thereby hangs a tale …

The original trust fund, ample though it may have seemed at the time, did not survive the ravages of the Second World War and the galloping inflation which followed. However, the Royal Automobile Club, which had taken a major role in administering the trophy from the outset, continued to finance the awards for many years without assistance from any other source.

The writer became involved as an *ad hoc* member of the committee advising on press and public relations and then when Leslie Webb, Chief Engineer of the RAC, retired as Secretary, was elected in his place.

Finance was a major consideration if the trophy was to continue in perpetuity and when Lady Segrave, who regularly attended the presentations, commented to the then chairman of the RAC, Wilfrid Andrews, that she hoped the trophy would never disappear into limbo, he was constrained to mention that it was only continuing through the good offices of the RAC. She promptly offered to provide for the future of the trophy in her will.

Whether or not Lady Segrave misunderstood the situation, or did not make the matter clear to her solicitor, it was revealed in her will that she had set up a trust fund, the proceeds of which should go to the *winners* of the Segrave

Trophy, which, of course, was useless in terms of ensuring the continuance of the award although a nice little nest-egg for the recipients. Although Lady Segrave's intentions had been clear enough there was apparently no way the terms of the will could be set aside so the RAC continued to provide the necessary finance.

There came a time when a great reorganization of the RAC took place, new activities were introduced, existing activities expanded and some dropped. In the uncertain gestation period of these plans, Nelson Mills Baldwin, Secretary-General of the RAC at the time, came to me and being aware of my enthusiasm for the Segrave, suggested that the time had come to seek a sponsor.

This was in 1978. Derek Guy, then Public Affairs Director of Castrol and a former competition motor-cyclist, takes up the story:

> We were talking in the Long Bar at the RAC when you suggested I might care to sponsor the Trophy. I said, *Yes, I will do it* and you seemed rather surprised that I made an on-the-spot decision. The reason for the quick response was that Castrol and Lord Wakefield had been so involved with record-breaking that there was no doubt in my mind that it was the right thing to do. Also Captain G. E. T. Eyston, OBE, MC, who won the Trophy in 1935 was a Director of Castrol.
>
> I had the pleasure of working with him in connection with his book and again at the Castrol Great Motoring Extravaganza at Olympia. When the Marquess Camden died in 1984, I became chairman of the committee.

The Castrol sponsorship took the trophy through another decade but then changes of direction at the oil company led to their relinquishing their connection.

We were very lucky. Trying to think of the ideal sponsor for such an award, the name of Ford came to mind. The Ford Motor Company had done more for British motor sport in modern times than any other company. Their rally cars had won all over the world (and been awarded a Segrave Trophy in the process); they had helped to create the most successful Grand Prix engine of all time and the popular Formula Ford had been used to train hundreds of aspiring racing-drivers.

A word with another old friend, Harry Calton, Ford's Public Affairs manager, reinforced by a letter from Jeffrey Rose, chairman of the RAC, to Derek Barron, chairman of Ford, and once again the Segrave Trophy had a most sympathetic sponsor, the best kind of sponsor, a sponsor who firmly believes in the endeavour he is supporting and is not doing it for purely commercial reasons.

In April 1988 the Ford Motor Company took over from Castrol and Derek Barron was elected to the Chair.

Apart from these changes in sponsorship, trustees and committee members, the original conditions are substantially unaltered. Winners do not receive miniatures of the trophy but a handsome plaque executed by the original sculptor, Gilbert Bayes; the committee does not necessarily meet in January but at convenient times; and if medals are thought to be appropriate, the winner is first asked for his or her views.

The only alteration to the conditions that can possibly affect the destination of the trophy in any year concerns the apparatus used. It is no longer practical to insist that cars, planes and boats be a hundred per cent British. Foreign parts are sometimes used by British manufacturers just as British parts are used by foreign manufacturers. So a clause has been added, 'The use of foreign apparatus need not necessarily exclude from the award but shall be taken into consideration where candidates and their achievements appear to be of equal merit.'

Although, obviously, the number of leading contenders and the strength of the opposition varies from year to year, the extent to which the machines used are of foreign manufacture can thus affect the issue when it is a tight race and there is little to choose between two or more nominees.

Almost certainly that very gallant lady, Sheila Scott, who died so tragically from cancer, might well have won the trophy had her record-breaking planes not been almost a hundred per cent foreign.

So might World Sports Car Champion Derek Bell had his car not been a German Porsche. Later, Martin Brundle was to win the championship *and* the Segrave but he was driving a British Jaguar.

Every year, however many the candidates, whatever the

apparatus they have used, all likely lads and lasses are carefully considered and their achievements put under close scrutiny. Sometimes, one stands high above all others, more often there are two or three nominees with little between them. Whatever the situation every year brings proof that the *Spirit of Adventure* lives on, just as it did in Segrave's day.

Postscript

More than fifty years after Segrave's death on Windermere, the last 't' of that tragedy was crossed, the last 'i' dotted …

A pensioner of the Castrol Company, living in Evesham, wrote to his former employers to the effect that in Portishead Churchyard, near Bristol, there was a grave in an unkempt state. The headstone indicated that it had been donated by Lord Wakefield, founder of the company. Under the circumstances should not the company see that the grave was properly maintained? Oh yes, he added, the name on the headstone is Victor Halliwell.

The name meant nothing to the man receiving the letter. In all probability he had not been born at the time of Segrave's death. So he checked on the company records. No Victor Halliwell.

A visit to Portishead threw some light on the matter. The epitaph showed that Victor Halliwell had died on Lake Windermere on 13 June 1930 'while upholding the honour and prestige of his country', and a circular plaque depicted a flying-boat and a speedboat named *Miss England II*.

The investigator knew about Segrave and his speedboat but he still did not know where Halliwell fitted into the picture. He went to the Rector of Portishead, the Reverend Nigel Eva, but he had only just moved to the parish and was unable to help.

The next call was to the offices of the *South Avon Mercury* in nearby Clevedon, a weekly paper which had been in existence for over a hundred years – and the copy for 21 June 1930 was produced almost immediately.

It revealed that Victor Halliwell was the Rolls-Royce engine test engineer responsible for the power-plant of *Miss*

England II. An employee of Rolls-Royce for five years, he had obtained a BSc degree in Automative Engineering at the Merchant Venturers College in Bristol.

His responsibilities ended when the engines were started and running efficiently but he had readily accepted Sir Henry's invitation to ride in the boat with him and Michael Wilcocks.

On such slender threads are lives saved and lost.

The newspaper account also revealed that when Halliwell's body was recovered from the dark waters he was still clutching his notebook and pencil – taking data on his beloved engines right to the end.

2 *The Trail-blazers*

The 1930s were exciting times in aviation. Just as centuries before, the great Portuguese navigators, Magellan, Vasco da Gama and their like had charted the oceans and opened up the great trade routes, so a new breed of adventurers took to the skies, often in primitive machines – not much more than string and paper – and blazed trails which would lead to the modern-day network of airline routes criss-crossing landmasses and oceans alike and linking the major cities of the world.

One such adventurer was a tough-looking, beaky-nosed Australian named Charles Kingsford-Smith. 'Smithy' to his Aussie pals. On 19 September 1930, flying a Sports Avian *Southern Cross Junior*, he touched down at Port Darwin in the Northern Territories of Australia, having set a new record for London–Australia flights with a time of 9 days, 21 hrs and 40 mins.

For this and his earlier transatlantic flight he was knighted by King George V and became the very first winner of the new Segrave Trophy.

In many ways Smithy, often described as the greatest of all air record-breakers, was a man ahead of his time.

He had a vision and that vision was of a Pacific Ocean straddled by safe and regular air routes over which giant air-liners would transport thousands of people and tons of freight in speed and safety. He nearly lost his life proving that it was more than a dream.

When he took off from Oakland, California, two years prior to his London–Australia flight, in a bid to cross the Pacific, that mighty ocean had not been flown at all. Several pilots had attempted it; all had lost their lives.

Not surprisingly in the context of the times, many people regarded Kingsford-Smith as a madman embarking upon a suicide flight. Yet he was a careful planner and was flying a good and proven plane, a three-engined Fokker F.VIIb monoplane christened, so no one could doubt the Aussie background of the venture, *Southern Cross*. As the Allied Forces knew to their cost, the German Air Force in the Great War owed much to the aircraft designed and built by the brilliant Dutchman, Anthony Fokker.

Smithy intended to cross the Pacific in three stages, the first to Honolulu, the second – equivalent to crossing the Atlantic – to Fiji and the final 1,500 miles to his home town of Brisbane.

Understandably aerial navigation in those days owed much to maritime practice. Instruments were not of today's scope, complexity and efficiency and there was no radar. So, 28 hours after take-off, it was with a sense of relief that the crew of the *Southern Cross* saw the volcanic islands of Hawaii loom through the clouds and a flock of American fighters take up station to escort them to land. By the time they touched down their fuel was dangerously low. Smithy's calculations had been correct – but only just.

The next leg to Fiji involved a flight of more than 3,000 miles over an area notorious for hurricanes, vicious and terrifying storms bringing in their wake death and destruction. Where cockleshell heroes had survived in tiny sailing ships, the crew of *Southern Cross* had no intention of surrender. The storms came and battered the aircraft but the skill of the crew and the genius of Fokker enabled the plane to absorb all that the elements could throw against them and the *Southern Cross* droned steadily on. There was one incident in the blackness of the night which could have proved fatal – all the lights on the instrument panel failed and there was no way of telling if they were on course. Fortunately, co-pilot Charles Ulm produced a pocket torch and by its slender beam they were able to read the instruments and follow a correct path.

The remainder of the 35-hour hop was comparatively uneventful, the most dangerous moment coming when they tried to land at Suva on Fiji.

For once Smithy's planning had gone astray and he had not

allowed for Suva's tiny landing strip, only 400 yards long. He circled it twice, thinking out his course of action, then cut the throttle and banked towards the field. The plane was going much too fast. The wheels bounced halfway along the strip and it seemed certain to the onlookers that it would plough into the fence and trees directly in its path but Smithy, tired as he was, saw that there was a patch of open ground to his right. Incredibly, he ground-looped his aircraft, missed the fence by a few feet and came safely to rest on the open space.

The last leg appeared to be easy: instead it took 20 hours to cover the 1,500 miles. Violent thunderstorms, lightning, strong winds, heavy rain, extreme cold and a dodgy compass all threatened to thwart them just as success was in their grasp but finally the sun came and with it the Eastern seaboard of Australia. They landed at Brisbane to a hero's welcome, the first men to fly across the Pacific.

Sadly for Smithy and Ulm the next few years were to bring more heartaches and disappointments than tangible reward. It was a time of financial crisis throughout the world and their efforts to introduce regular air services foundered for lack of support. There was a period when Smithy was reduced to taking people on air joy-rides at ten shillings a time. He was also involved in an ill-fated attempt to manufacture an all-Australian motor-car, again named *Southern Cross*.

In December 1934 Charles Ulm took off in a bid to break the Pacific record. He was never seen or heard of again. Somewhere over that vast ocean he must have run into trouble and his aircraft plunged beneath the waves, never to be found.

That year Smithy fell from grace with some of his countrymen. The England–Australia Air Race was held, probably the most fantastic air race of all time, and it was won in record time by the Englishmen, C. W. A. Scott and Tom Campbell Black, flying a De Havilland Comet, *Grosvenor House*. (Scott had been the first to fly solo from Australia in a Gipsy Moth in 1931.)

Smithy did not take part and his fellow Australians could not understand why. They felt let down. The previous year – 1933 – he had set a new England–Australia record of 7 days,

4 hrs, 50 mins in a Percival Gull, designed and built by another Australian, Edgar Percival, who had settled in England. Now Smithy had let the Poms snatch that record away from him without a fight.

Smithy could have given them several reasons why he had not taken part in the air race, every one of them a good one. But he was not the sort of man to make excuses or justify his actions or inaction, come to that. Yet there is no doubt that he was both hurt and stung by the criticism. He was thirty-eight years of age and a sick man but he determined on one last record flight. He would beat Scott and Black's time of 71 hours and really give his critics something to talk about.

The flight started well. At Allabahad he was slightly behind Scott's time but he and his co-pilot, Tommy Petherbridge, were feeling fairly confident since the Comet had been affected by engine trouble over the second part of the route so that if the Aussies could keep going as they were they should be on schedule to beat the Englishmen's time.

It was not to be. After take-off from Allabahad no one ever saw them again. Somewhere over the treacherous Bay of Bengal Smithy's Lockheed disappeared. Two years later a wheel from the plane was washed up on the Burmese coast, the only trace ever found of the plane and its gallant crew.

Today giant airliners transport millions of passengers to all corners of the globe, covering millions of air miles to do so. It would be nice to think that, every now and again, one of those passengers would think of Charles Kingsford-Smith and Charles Ulm, two men who shared a dream. Every passenger carried today, every mile flown, is a tribute to their memory.

Kingsford-Smith was one of a number of Australians who played prominent roles in the trail-blazing days of aviation. Another was the man whose London–Australia record Smithy beat, 'Bert' Hinkler, and Hinkler was to be the second recipient of the Segrave Trophy.

The list of those who have won the Segrave Trophy provides a gallery of truly remarkable men and women. Some of them have stories which are unique even in such illustrious company. One such was Herbert John Louis Hinkler, AFC, DSM – although today he is not remembered to the extent some of the Segrave winners are.

Born in wonderfully named Bundaberg, Queensland, in 1892, he built a glider at the age of fourteen. The noteworthy aspect of this was *not* that the glider failed to fly but that in 1906, when the story of flight was in its infancy, anyone should think of building a glider, let alone a lad of fourteen. But this was no schoolboy fantasy. Five years later he built another – and this one did fly. At this time, Bert had yet to see his first aircraft, a situation remedied the following year when 'Wizard' Stone, legendary for his flying displays as he 'barnstormed' Australasia, showed up in Bundaberg with a Bleriot plane.

There weren't too many fliers and would-be fliers around at the time so not surprisingly the footloose pilot and the air-struck youngster got on famously. Bert worked on the machine with Stone and when the 'Wizard' left for a barnstorming tour of New Zealand he went along too. Flying such a primitive machine was not a job holding out long-term prospects and, after some hairy moments, the Bleriot almost inevitably crashed badly enough to terminate the tour – although, fortunately, not the pilot.

Hinkler eventually set sail for the Old Country, landing at Grimsby during Easter, 1914. He soon found a job, working for pioneer aircraft manufacturer, T. O. M. Sopwith, at Kingston. But war was in the offing and he soon found himself Leading Mechanic Hinkler, HLJ of the Royal Naval Air Service. It was inconceivable that someone who had already shown such a keen interest in the air would be content just working on the engines of planes which someone else would fly, so in 1915 Hinkler was delighted when he was posted to Whitley as an observer, flying anti-Zeppelin patrols.

Early in 1917 he was posted to Dunkirk as a gunner-observer and made 122 flights over enemy lines, shooting down at least four enemy aircraft, for which he was awarded the Distinguished Service Medal.

Although he had been flying for some three years continuously it was always with someone else at the controls so one can imagine his joy when he was informed that he was being sent to Eastbourne for flying training. He passed out in July 1918 and was sent to the Italian Front, flying Sopwith

Camels and being demobilized at the end of the war with the rank of lieutenant, Royal Air Force.

He had no intention of giving up flying now and obtained Civil Licence No. 48. He planned to fly solo to Australia in ten days with hops of 1,000 to 1,500 miles and had negotiated with Sopwith for a Sopwith Dove, fitted with an 80 hp Rhone engine. With a long-range tank located in the front cockpit he figured to have enough fuel to enable him to accomplish the various stages of his flight with ease. When the Australian government offered £10,000 prize money for the first Australians to fly home in an aircraft designed and built in the British Commonwealth, Hinkler could not believe his luck. He was a good pilot. His Dove was as British as they come and no one could deny that a native of Bundaberg was Australian.

It came like a bolt from the blue: his entry was refused. But there was nothing sinister in it at all. What had happened was that an uncharted section of the England–Australia route, that section from Calcutta to Darwin, had now been surveyed by Brigadier-General Borton and Captain Ross Smith and their report to the Air Ministry set the alarm bells ringing. They warned that there was frequent bad weather in the region, often severe enough to force down planes – and that there was a remarkable absence of anywhere to land. Their conclusion and firm recommendation was that no plane should fly over it unless it had a *minimum* range of 2,000 miles and this, of course, effectively ruled out Hinkler's Dove.

Bert had long since learned to take the rough with the smooth. He moved on to A. V. Roe as test pilot, remaining with that firm for seven years. One of the company's products was the Baby, a sturdy little aircraft, powered with a 35 hp Green engine of pre-war design and cruising at 65 to 70 m.p.h.

On 31 May 1920, Hinkler took off from Croydon in a prototype Baby, destination Rome. Over the Alps his oil was running low and eventually he was forced to land at Turin, touching down less than nine hours after leaving London. His time for the 650-mile flight was a new non-stop solo record and he was awarded the Britannia Trophy, the first civilian to receive it. It was to become a habit. He was awarded it three times in all.

The whole world now knew about the Avro Baby and Bert took the record-breaker to Australia *by sea*, selling it there after an aerial promotional tour of his native land.

Back in England, he tested the new Avro Avian, which was to prove quite a plane, and flew in various competitions for Avro with some success. The international speed contest for the Schneider Trophy was focusing a lot of attention on sea-planes and Hinkler was roped in to do the final acceptance tests on the Short Crusader.

The 1925 Schneider Trophy was to be held in Baltimore, USA, and Avro loaned Hinkler to the British team as pilot for the reserve plane, a Gloster III-A.

Britain's No. 1, Biard, the world sea-plane record-holder, crashed just ten days before the race and Hinkler, with less than thirty minutes' flying time on his machine, was called into the team. In story books, Bert would have led the team to glory and won the race, but it didn't quite work out like that.

On race morning, 26 October, Hinkler took off for final navigability trials. The water was very choppy – three footers – and when he returned to base and touched down, one of the Gloster's floats burst and that was the end of Bert's Schneider Trophy chances.

Not all was lost. Broad, De Havilland's test pilot, flying the other Gloster III-A, finished second in the race to the great American flier, Lt Jimmy Doolittle (Curtiss B3C-2) and in so doing broke the British sea-plane 100-km closed-circuit record.

Hinkler was next in the news in 1927 when he flew an Avian to Riga on a test flight, covering 1,200 miles in 10½ hours for a non-stop solo record which earned him a medal from the Latvian government, grateful if surprised at having been put on the map by an Aussie from Bundaberg.

Hinkler was still set on breaking the Australian record but the climate was not good for such endeavours. In the wake of Charles Lindbergh's solo flight across the Atlantic in the *Spirit of St Louis* there was a surge of long-distance air record attempts, most of them failures and some resulting in the deaths of the participants.

Confronted with this lack of enthusiasm on the part of wealthy backers, Hinkler decided to make a bid relying on his own resources.

He chose the Avro Avian 581 for the flight. Originally designed and developed by Roy Chadwick for the 1926 *Daily Mail* Light Aeroplane Trials, it had a large wing area, low structural weight and folding wings, one of the conditions of the competition.

The prototype was fitted with a 70 hp Armstrong-Siddeley engine but after trials an 85 hp ADC Cirrus II engine was fitted and in this form was sold as the Type 581A, the first customer being Hinkler.

He went to work on it with a vengeance. He designed a wide track divided undercarriage which moved aft as the wings were folded. This lowered the engine, making one-man maintenance or repair a much more practical proposition. It also made movement on the ground easier. New wings were fitted, together with a metal airscrew and a steerable tail-wheel. A starter operated from the cockpit was installed, a 66-gallon long-range tank fitted into the front cockpit and a dinghy and paddle (last resort?) stowed under the turtle-decking behind the pilot. Thus modified and equipped the plane was known as Type 581E, the 'E' presumably being for 'Experimental'.

The intrepid Aussie took off from Croydon on 7 February 1928 and landed at Darwin on the 22nd, his time of 15 days, 11 hrs, 7 mins constituting a record. It was the first light-aeroplane flight to Australia, the first solo flight to Australia, and in passing Hinkler had also broken the London–Rome record.

An ecstatic Australia made him an honorary squadron-leader in the Royal Australian Air Force (it was said he never got around to wearing the uniform) and awarded him the Air Force Cross. He was also awarded the Britannia Trophy for the second time and the Gold Medal of the Fédération Aeronautique Internationale.

A man like Hinkler could no more rest on his laurels than Tom could stop chasing Jerry. In 1931 he broke new territory, flying a De Havilland Puss Moth from New York to London via Jamaica, Venezuela, Trinidad, Brazil, West Africa, Spain and France – a potent demonstration of the great possibilities for light aircraft and the first solo crossing of the South Atlantic. It was enough to make him the second Australian flier to win the Segrave Trophy and it also earned him the Royal Aero Club's Gold Medal.

But nagging away at him was the thought that the London–Australia record was no longer his. He wanted it back and in 1933, he set off on another attempt. He had used up his luck. He crashed during a snowstorm over the Appenine Mountains and his body was not found until four days later.

Fifty years to the day after Hinkler's record flight to Australia, Flight-Lieutenant David Cyster, an instructor of the Hunter Squadron at No. 4 Flying School, RAF Station Valley, took off from Dunsfold, Surrey, in a Tiger Moth, his destination, Sydney, Australia, his purpose to commemorate the Golden Jubilee of Hinkler's epic flight. Cyster took twice as long as Hinkler had done. In Bert's day, fliers were usually assured of a welcome where the map was coloured red and a lot of it was; today, politics, wars, insurrections and more red tape than red maps can be a pilot's nightmare, especially for the solo flier.

Hinkler's record-breaking plane went to Brisbane Museum but his fellow-countrymen paid him a unique tribute in 1983, fifty years after his death.

They went to Southampton, purchased the house *Mon Repos* where he had lived with his English wife, packed up every brick and timber and took the house back with them to Australia where it was rebuilt as the star attraction in the Bundaberg Bi-Centennial Celebrations.

Bundaberg's most famous native son had come home.

In those years leading up to the Second World War, heady years in aviation history, several women pilots were among the nominees for the Segrave Trophy.

Foremost was Amy Johnson, eldest of four daughters born to the wife of a Hull fish-merchant. Working in London as a typist in a solicitor's office and living in a bed-sitter in Maida Vale, she took flying lessons at the London Aeroplane Club, based at Stag Lane, allegedly to occupy her mind after an unhappy love affair. The cost was £2 an hour while under instruction, £1.50 (or 30 shillings as it was then) flying solo and the club's chief instructor estimated that the average pupil took 8–12 hours to learn. It may sound very inexpensive today but at that time when someone earning £5 per week was well-paid it was quite a pricey business.

She had her first lesson in 1928, was told by the instructor that she was 'absolutely hopeless' and went solo some ten months later. She followed up by becoming the first woman in Britain to take a ground engineer's licence and by that time had her heart set on a career in aviation. The feminists who now complain in the eighties about 'male chauvinism' and 'sexist attitudes' should have been around in the thirties …

Confiding her ambitions to her chief instructor, Captain V. H. Baker, Amy was told bluntly that she would have to find some way of winning her spurs 'by flying to Australia, for instance'. If that was supposed to deter Amy, Captain Baker had picked the wrong person. She took him literally and immediately made plans to do just as he had suggested, whether or not he had meant it.

She acquired a De Havilland Gypsy Moth which was already fitted with long-range tanks, giving it a duration of approximately thirteen hours. That was about the limit of the special equipment fitted to *Jason*, as Amy christened her prize new possession, and there was no radio. She took with her an air-cushion, a parachute, a sheath-knife, a revolver and her childhood teddy bear, and set off for Australia in May 1930. She landed there 19½ days later, having survived heat, fog, bad weather, torrential rain, shortage of fuel, a crash at Rangoon, forced landings, engine trouble and reports in the world press of 'Lone Girl Flyer Missing'.

She returned to London on August Bank Holiday, 1930, a passenger on a British airliner. Two hundred thousand people waited to greet her at Croydon Aerodome – she was the most famous woman in the world.

She was soon engaged upon her next flight – to Peking. It was a failure. She crashed in thick fog 50 miles from Warsaw with the Great Wall of China a long, long way away. Undaunted, she planned a flight to Tokyo in a two-seater biplane, accompanied by Jack Humphries, the chief ground engineer at Stag Lane. They reached Moscow in one day, the first time anyone had covered the 1,760 miles in twenty-four hours or less, and Tokyo in ten days, breaking the light plane record.

As splendid an achievement as it was, the Tokyo flight did not make the impact it might have done because almost simultaneously a young aviator two years Amy's junior, James Allan Mollison, flying solo in a Puss Moth, had broken the record from London to Australia by two days.

Amy had met him briefly in Australia at the conclusion of her flight there. Now she sent him a telegram of congratulation. Events moved swiftly. In March 1932, Mollison took off from Lympne on his way to break the England–Capetown record; in July he and Amy were married at St George's, Hanover Square; and in August he became the first flier to cross the Atlantic solo from east to west in his Gipsy-engined Puss Moth.

Amy had also had designs on the Atlantic but instead turned her attentions to South Africa. Her record flight from London to Capetown *and back* earned her the Segrave Trophy.

A measure of the merit of her achievement was that in the same year other contenders for the trophy were her husband, Jim Mollison, with two record-breaking flights; Kaye Don who, following in Segrave's footsteps, broke the World Water Speed Record with a convincing 119 m.p.h. in *Miss England III*; and George Eyston who, in his Magic Midget, became the first man to exceed two miles a minute in a baby car, clocking 120.56 m.p.h.

Kaye Don's boat was owned by Lord Wakefield who spent the then vast sum of £40,000 on the record bid. It was the nearest Don would come to the Segrave Trophy, his later attempts on the World Land Speed Record in *Silver Bullet* ending in failure. For Eyston, however, it would be a different story …

Four years after her trophy-winning record Amy Johnson was to repeat her feat in the ubiquitous Percival Gull and that 1936 record would stand for thirty-one years until, in 1967, Sheila Scott beat it.

The marriage of the world's two most famous aviators was not to last. Jim Mollison, who had been engaged to Lady Diana Wellesley, great-grand-daughter of the Duke of

Wellington, prior to his wedding to Amy, had something of a reputation as a playboy. He had been in the headlines for a variety of exploits, not all of them connected with flying. He was fined for assault after a scrap in Mayfair in the small hours and featured prominently in the Melbourne papers after beating up a man who insulted him. Four years in the RAF and five years' commercial flying had added extra toughness to this rugged Glaswegian who had few illusions about himself: 'Other pilots fly until the petrol runs out,' he once said, 'I fly till the brandy runs out.'

Reluctantly Amy had to face the truth that Jim had spent much of their married life philandering or drinking. In 1938 they were divorced.

In 1940 they met again. Both had joined the Air Transport Auxiliary, the unit which ferried warplanes to the operational zones. It seems probable that Amy still had strong feelings for her ex-husband from remarks she made to friends and letters she wrote at the time.

They might, perhaps, have got together again – Jim's second marriage also went adrift – but Fate took a hand. In January, 1941, in foggy weather, the plane Amy was ferrying crashed into the Thames Estuary. It is believed that Amy baled out but, trapped in her parachute lines, drowned before help could reach her. It was ironic that a girl who had flown over the Atlantic and the Pacific, the storm-wracked Bay of Biscay and the terrifying Indian Ocean, should perish within sight of Southend Pier.

Some light was thrown on the mystery by Dr W. T. K. Cody who said,

> I was medical officer in HMS *Berkeley* and on that day we were escorting a convoy into the Thames Estuary. We had been heavily bombed and at one time counted eight parachutes in the air. A plane crashed near us and, as it remained floating, the First Lieutenant and I went across in the ship's boat; the plane was half-full of water but otherwise empty except for a suitcase which we took back to the ship.
>
> It was only when I opened it and found Amy Mollison's logbook that we knew who had died. As a postscript, the captain of, I think, one of our minesweepers saw a body in the water and dived in from the bridge. He was only in the water

for about twenty minutes but he died shortly after he was picked up.

Amy Johnson was only 38 when she died and who knows what she might have achieved when peace returned. To this day she remains Britain's most famous woman pilot. The King had given her the CBE, there was a popular song called 'Amy, Our Wonderful Amy' (accolade indeed!) and a stage musical entitled simply *Amy*. Her home town, the city of Hull, always an enterprising place, issued a commemorative stamp. An Amy Johnson Memorial Scholarship was instituted to enable other women to pursue careers in aviation.

In May 1980, a 1930 Gypsy Moth took off from Croydon to commemorate Amy's Australian flight half-a-century earlier. Let the pilot of that plane, Sue Thompson, have the last word: 'She was a pioneer who changed flying for all women ever since.'

Jim Mollison, who might so easily have been a Segrave winner himself, survived the war, more flights, a lot of bright lights and a handful of fights, to die in 1959 at the age of fifty-four.

Amy and Jim could have been one of the world's great love stories: instead it ended in tragedy. Amy at least is remembered. Sadly, Jim's land-based escapades have tended to obscure recognition of his very real achievements in the air.

After Amy Johnson, the next flier to be awarded the Segrave Trophy was Ken Waller in 1934. He flew from Australia to England and from Belgium to the Belgian Congo and back in a De Havilland Comet. The aircraft belonged to a man better known in motor-racing – Bernard Rubin, who was one of the legendary 'Bentley Boys' and a winner of the Le Mans 24-Hour Race.

Waller eventually settled in South Africa and is the only trophy winner of whom the organizers have lost all trace.

There is, however, a sad little footnote to his story provided by the New Zealander Eoin Young, bibliophile and motoring writer, who says:

Oddly enough I was offered Waller's special Segrave Trophy plaque in its velvet-lined presentation case by a dealer in Arundel a few years ago. He wasn't sure what it was or who K. A. Waller was and to my chagrin, I didn't know either. By the time I had established Waller's identity the plaque had been sold.

Meanwhile, an attractive New Zealand woman, Jean Gardner Batten, had embarked upon a record-breaking career which was to bring her five important records and four world records for any type of aeroplane. She made the fastest-ever journey from England to South America in 61 hrs, 15 mins, and in so doing became the first woman to fly the South Atlantic Ocean. She was awarded the CBE.

She flew from England to Australia to make the fastest solo flight for the route in 5 days, 21 hrs, and continued on to New Zealand to complete the first-ever solo flight from England to that country in 11 days, 1 hr, 25 mins. For this and the South Atlantic flight she was awarded the Segrave Trophy.

Jean gilded the lily by breaking the solo record from Darwin to London on her return flight. Apart from the CBE and the Segrave Trophy, she was the first woman to be awarded the medal of the Fédération Aeronautique Internationale, was given the Légion d'honneur by France and the Southern Cross by Brazil. In her native land she was hailed as 'New Zealand's Ambassador of the Skies'.

The aircraft she used was Percival Gull G-ADPR which, at the outbreak of the Second World War, was pressed into service by the RAF who used it on communications work. It was returned to the Percival Company in 1946 and then in 1961 was handed over to the Shuttleworth Collection for safe-keeping. For a few years thereafter it was flown at various air displays but by 1969 its active flying career was over. In 1978 it was decided to restore the Gull to its former glory and an appeal was launched to raise the necessary funds.

As for Jean herself, she published her story, *My Life*, in 1938 and the then Secretary of State for Air, the Marquis of Londonderry, said:

The Segrave Trophy

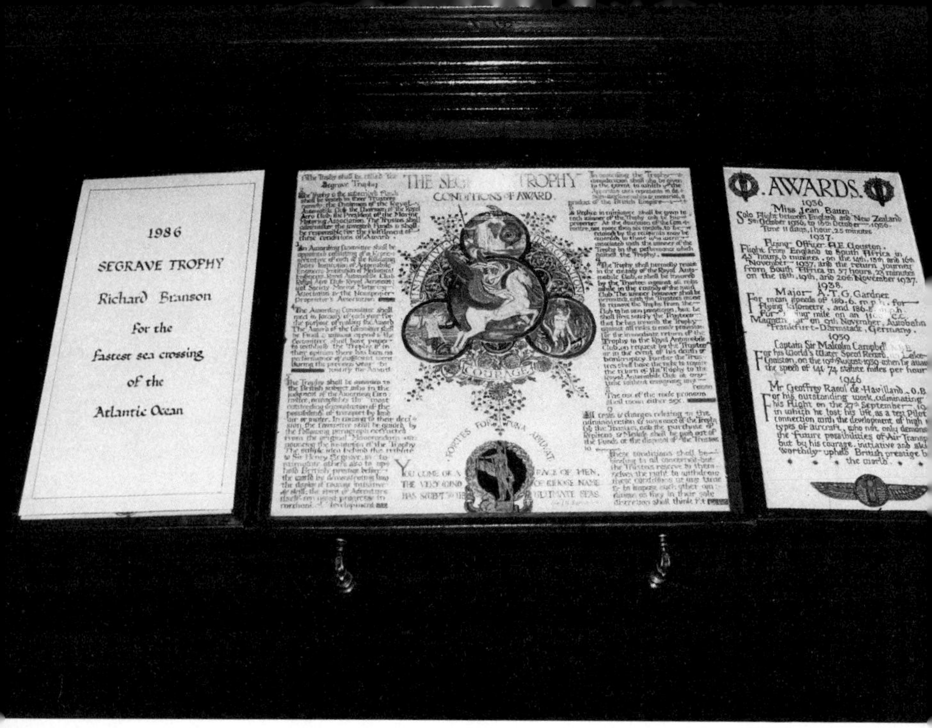

Conditions of the award of the trophy and its winners are featured on illuminated scrolls contained in the plinth of the trophy

Sir Henry Segrave, whose portrait hangs in the RAC at Pall Mall, London. The cigarette in his left hand would doubtless meet with disapproval today!

Derek Barron, present chairman of the Segrave Awarding Committee

Segrave's Golden Arrow at Daytona Beach, Florida, where a new World Land Speed Record of 231 m.p.h. was set

The Golden Arrow at the Sunbeam works minus the side fairings and tail which were fitted for the successful record attempt

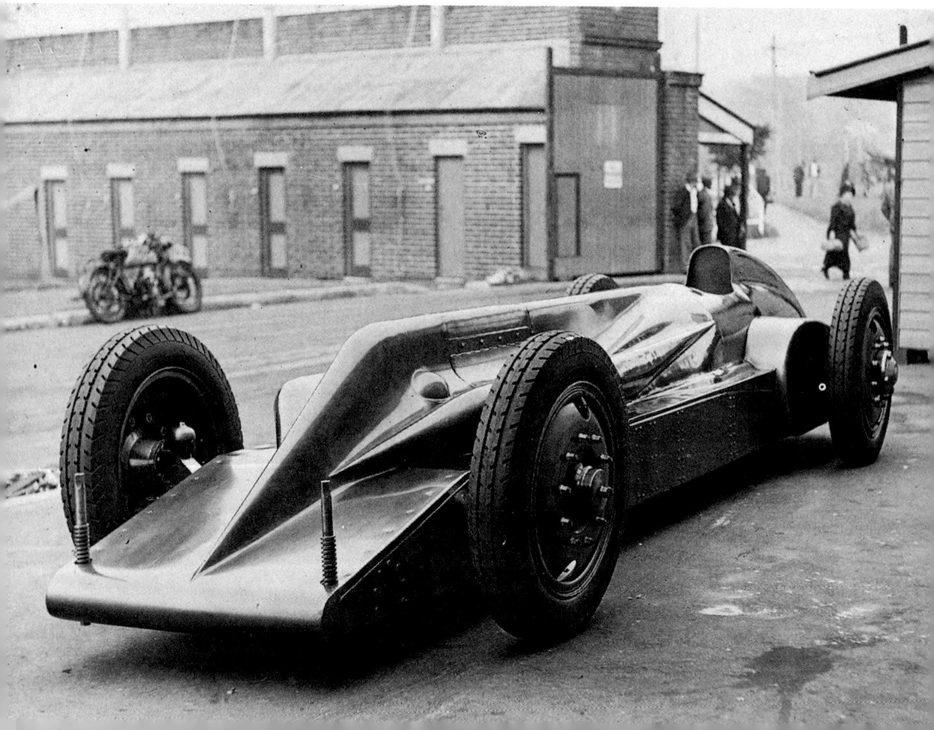

A parade of record-breakers. *Left to right*: the Sunbeam driven by 'Bill' Lee Guinness; Segrave's 1927 Sunbeam; and the Golden Arrow, this time fitted with smooth side fairings

Robert Horne breaking the UK Flying Mile Record in his 512M Ferrari Special

The de Havilland Comet in which C.W.A. Scott and Tom Campbell-Black won the greatest air race of them all – England to Australia, 1934

Three great winners of the Segrave Trophy. *Left to right:* Test pilot and wartime ace fighter John Cunningham; long-distance air record-breaker Jean Batten; and world motor-cycling champion Geoff Duke

Intrepid airwoman Sheila Scott with the plane in which she took 100 World Class Records between 1965 and 1971

Eve Jackson with the tiny microlight aircraft in which she flew from England to Australia, the first person to do so in this type of plane

Peter Twiss with his Segrave plaque and the Segrave Trophy awarded him in 1957 for breaking the World Air Speed Record at 1,132 m.p.h.

> Miss Batten has demonstrated that, given the good fortune of overcoming what we might call the major risks of weather and mechanical difficulties, she left nothing to chance in the way of inspection of her aeroplane and attention to the minor points of detail, which are the hallmark of the good and experienced pilot. As a navigator she is in my judgment second to none.

Jean eventually retired to the Canaries but in 1977 she was officially invited home to open 'The Pioneers of New Zealand Aviation' Pavilion at the Museum of Transport and Technology, first stage of a memorial project for Sir Keith Park, who played a major role in the Battle of Britain and who died on 6 February 1975.

Park was a remarkable man who landed at Gallipoli in the Great War as a 22-year-old lance-corporal and was commissioned in the field. He joined the Royal Flying Corps and was decorated several times – Military Cross and Bar, Distinguished Flying Cross and the French Croix de Guerre. He remained in the service when peace came and in 1937 was ADC to King George VI at his Coronation. Appointed to command No. 11 Fighter Group in 1940 he was one of the 'few' who bore the brunt of the Battle of Britain and saved the country from German invasion. Later he became Commander, Allied Forces in Egypt; Commander Allied Air Forces, Malta; Air Officer Commanding Middle East; and, finally, Allied Commander-in-Chief, South-East Asia.

Jean wrote to me:

> I was so impressed by the enthusiasm of all concerned in trying to raise the money to construct a World War Two airfield and link it by electric tramway to the Museum that I decided to stay on for several months and help raise funds for the project.
>
> My efforts culminated in a banquet for almost 1,000 guests at which I was introduced by the Governor-General, Sir Denis Blundell, and thanked after my address by the Prime Minister, the Rt. Hon. Robert Muldoon. It was a great success and raised a clear 9,000 dollars for the fund.

That banquet, entitled 'A Tribute to Courage' was indicative of the esteem in which Jean was held in her native land, a land where 13,000 commemorative covers were issued to mark the fortieth anniversary of her record England–New Zealand flight and where the postal franking 'Auckland East' has been replaced by 'Jean Batten Place'.

It would be forty-four years before another woman won the Segrave Trophy – Lady Arran in 1980 – but Jean Batten, still a vivacious woman at seventy-one, would still be around.

There was another woman among the trail-blazing pilots who were contenders for the Segrave in the 1930s – Mrs Beryl Markham, who crash-landed in her Percival Vega Gull after becoming the first woman to fly the North Atlantic solo east to west in 1936.

Beryl was a typical character of the times and fifty years on she would be portrayed as a *femme fatale* in the film *White Mischief*, which exposed the scandalous lives of the society set in East Africa between the wars. Whatever else happened in her life, Beryl was a dare-devil airwoman and, like Sheila Scott later, may be counted unlucky not to have won the Segrave.

Other fliers in the running in the 1930s, apart from Jim Mollison, were J. Broadbent who, in 1937, flying a De Havilland Leopard Moth, broke the England–Australia solo record; Sir Alan Cobham, who did much to improve the feasibility of long-distance passenger flights; the Marquess of Clydesdale (Westland PV3) and Flt Lt D. F. McIntyre (Westland Wallace), first to fly over Mount Everest (3 April 1933); and Flt Lt Llewellyn, who flew from England to South Africa in 1936 in a 35 hp Aeronca-JAP, the JAP being most famous as a motor-cycle and speedway engine.

The year 1937 saw the Segrave go to Flying-Officer A. E. Clouston for a solo flight from England to South Africa and back. He took 45 hrs, 6 mins on the outward journey, 57 hrs, 23 mins on the return.

The following year, accompanied by V. Ricketts, he flew from England to New Zealand and back in 10 days, 22 hrs.

Clouston would subsequently be promoted to Air Commodore, earn the CB, DSO, DFC and AFC, and retire, appropriately enough, to a house named 'Wings' in remote north Cornwall.

Many more airmen would win the Segrave Trophy but mostly in the role of test pilot. The day of the trail blazer had gone, or so it seemed.

Yet in 1987 the award of the trophy to one, Eve Jackson, brought all the old memories of the pioneers flooding back.

Not that her route was unusual, but her aircraft certainly was. She became the first person to fly a microlight, or ultra-lightweight, aircraft from England to Australia, the 12,000-mile odyssey taking fifteen months.

Her tiny, British-built Shadow monoplane, nicknamed *Gertie* after an aunt, weighed about 150 kilos and had a cruising speed of 36 m.p.h. It was manufactured by CFM Metal-Fax, of Leiston, Suffolk, and the head of the company, Dave Cook, a sturdy countryman with a dry sense of humour, was awarded a Segrave Medal, Eve giving him much of the credit for her epic journey.

Later Dave was to fly one of his microlights, which he calls *Shadows* as stunt pilot for the film *Slipstream* on location in Yorkshire and Turkey. The Turks were so impressed with the little 'pusher' plane that they ordered 100 armoured versions for patrolling the Syrian border.

In the first five years after Metal–Fax was founded in 1984 the factory produced 95 *Shadows* at £9,000–£15,000 apiece.

Twenty-nine-year-old Eve, a bouncy extrovert, mortgaged her home to make the trip and her feat was accomplished fifty-five years after Amy Johnson had won the trophy. Eve was also the first recipient of the trophy under its sponsorship by the Ford Motor Company.

She left Biggin Hill in Kent in April 1986 and touched down in Darwin, Australia, in June 1987. Down Under she was welcomed by her seventy-year-old father and a telegram from Prime Minister Margaret Thatcher.

During her flight, which she originally planned would take six months, she fought everything from natural elements to the red tape of the twenty-two countries through or over which she passed.

Her troubles began long before she cleared Europe. The weather was bad when she left Biggin Hill. In Czechoslovakia, the police in a rural area contemplated arresting her – presumably they thought she was a spy – and in Yugoslavia she was robbed of $700 while making a phone call – which makes Yugoslav calls even more expensive than British Telecom!

Cruising over the Greek border, she was shot at. 'I had been told to keep low because there was a military exercise going on,' she laughed, 'but when I saw bursts of fire coming from a ground battery and silver flashes in the sky I took a sharp left and put on full throttle.'

The Middle East, surprisingly, was more hospitable. When officials at the Syrian airport of Damascus saw the tiny matchstick in which she was flying they waived their usual high landing fees. And at Amman in Jordan she was hustled off to meet King Hussein who gave her an inscribed watch and offered sponsorship support.

Crossing the Saudi Arabian desert was something else again with the temperature a sizzling 125°F. An enforced delay of several weeks at Oman in the Persian Gulf did not help and when she eventually took off for Pakistan she faced a dangerous 200-mile sea-crossing since she was not allowed to fly over Iran. Hugging the coast, the journey took five hours and 'it was pretty scary'.

The engine in *Gertie* has only two cylinders and over Burma one of them failed. Eve had to make an emergency landing and then do the repair job herself. In Thailand she was forced to land at an air-force base and she was further delayed in Indonesia where she was refused permission to land on the island of Timor.

The last lap was a four-hour flight over the shark-infested ocean to Darwin, after which she flew on to Sydney.

In addition to the Segrave Trophy she became the first microlight pilot to be awarded the Gold Medal of the Royal Aeronautical Society and the first apprentice of the Guild of Air Pilots and Navigators, who also awarded her their Sword of Honour for her 'contribution to general aviation and particularly the microlight industry'.

Perhaps most amazing of all, Eve had only 106 hours of flying time when she set off on her epic journey.

Amy Johnson would have been proud of her.

3 *The Test Pilots*

For six years the skies, which once were empty save for the trail-blazing pioneers of the air, were filled with the clatter of machine guns and the drone of heavy bombers on their way to drop their deadly cargoes. When the Second World War ended and peace came, many wartime pilots turned to civil aviation, flying the routes which the Kingsford-Smiths, Hinklers and Johnsons had mapped out.

Some, like Air Vice-Marshal Don 'Pathfinder' Bennett, started their own companies and opened up new routes. The majority provided a pool of trained personnel for the established airlines and the burgeoning charter companies. A few became the nucleus of a new elite, men who would risk their lives in startling new aircraft of revolutionary concept and design in order to prove the craft's safety, or find its faults, before a single passenger was carried – the test pilots.

Their lives depended upon three factors: the designer being right; the materials sound; and the workmanship good. Sometimes, one or more of those factors was sadly adrift and sometimes test pilots paid with their lives, a risk that they weighed against the thousands of lives which might be saved by their tests, a risk they found worthwhile.

Test pilots come in all shapes and sizes: slim, plump, tall, short, fair, dark. Very few of them look like Flying-Officer Kite or even David Niven when risking all for Queen and Country and, mostly, they do not resemble the dashing pilots in boys' comics. Nine of them (at the present count) do have one thing in common, all have been recipients of the Segrave Trophy. Among them are Brian Trubshaw of Concorde fame, dark and chunky; Bill Bedford, rather like a bank manager;

and fair-haired, ruddy countenanced John Cunningham, who looks as if he is a happy farmer. Which perhaps is not too far from the truth since he is a keen gardener, grows his own fruit and vegetables and prides himself on his asparagus – which he also enjoys eating.

The first test pilot to be awarded the Segrave after the Second World War was the bearer of a famous name in aviation history, Geoffrey Raoul de Havilland, OBE. Alas, his award in 1946 was a posthumous one since he was killed on a test flight on 27 September of that year. The citation mentioned the value of the flight he was undertaking when he died and praised his outstanding work in connection with the development of high-speed aircraft, which had been a major step in demonstrating the possibilities of air transport for the years to come.

The next test pilot to be honoured, two years after De Havilland, was one of those with a distinguished combat record. Old Carthusian John Derry was eighteen when hostilities began and immediately volunteered for the RAF, serving for three years as a wireless operator/air gunner before being sent for pilot training. He was commissioned in 1942 and by the end of the war was a squadron-leader commanding No. 182 Squadron, equipped with Typhoon fighters.

He had earned the DFC and a Belgian decoration for bravery and had married a lovely girl, Eve. He also had a bullet wound in the thigh but it did not affect his flying and when the opportunity came of being a test pilot, the lean, fair-haired six-footer jumped at it. It was to lead to his becoming the first Briton to fly faster than sound. On 6 September 1948, flying a tailless De Havilland 108 from Hatfield, Herts, he broke the 100-km (60-mile) closed-circuit air record at a speed of 605.23 m.p.h. In so doing he broke through the 'sound-barrier' of 760 m.p.h. at sea level. People used to talk a lot about the sound-barrier in those days although most of them, including the present writer, didn't know what it was exactly. As one of the non-technically minded, about the only explanation I could follow ran something like this: When a plane flies below the speed of sound the air flows over, under and around it. At the speed of sound the air compresses and builds up in front of the aircraft. Then, when the plane goes faster than sound, shock waves travel out from the barrier and cause booms as they reach the ground.

Derry, the flier in the distinctive bow-tie, became a hero and a national figure. A film was put into motion, *The Sound Barrier*, and John was an idol of many small boys and not least two little girls – his children, Carol and Josephine.

The cruelties of Fate are often very hard to understand and the gods had a fiendish end in store for a brave and brilliant pilot ...

On 6 September 1956, four years to the day after he had first broken through the sound-barrier, Derry was scheduled to demonstrate the experimental De Havilland 110 to the crowds at the Farnborough Air Show.

The day started badly. The news came through that the aircraft had developed a fault and could not be started up. John and his observer, Tony Richard, had to go and collect the standby plane.

As far as the press were concerned it was to be a quiet day at the show. Most of the press angles had been fully exploited on the previous days of the show which had had a press preview on the Tuesday.

Mid-afternoon there were only three men in the press tent: Peter King, press officer of the show; Cyril Birks, air correspondent of the London *Evening News* and a one-time neighbour of mine; and my old friend and colleague Squadron-Leader Pat Gregory, then air correspondent of the Press Association.

Pat had certainly not intended to be there that afternoon.

> On the Friday – when by coincidence I had lunched with John Derry and some others – Bob Carrington, Acting News Editor, told me over the phone that he was worried about leaving a gap on Saturday and would I mind covering. I agreed although I didn't anticipate anything more arduous than a drink or two with the mates.

Just before 4 p.m., 120,000 people, eager to see and hear the sound-barrier broken, craned their necks skywards as the DH110 appeared overhead. From 40,000 feet Derry put the machine into a high-speed dive and seconds later the double clap of man-made thunder echoed across the countryside as the plane overtook the noise of its own engines.

Inside the press tent, Gregory phoned the news that Derry had broken the sound-barrier again.

In the skies above, Derry levelled out and raced towards the runway at 500 feet. The plane, weakened by the high-speed dive, literally disintegrated, giving the crew not a chance.

One of the two engines, more than a ton of metal, scythed into the crowd, killing 29 people and injuring another 60. Pat Gregory:

> I put the phone down, walked outside the press tent and saw a piece of wreckage hurtle past just about 20 feet away. I got back to the office and spent the next three or four hours dictating copy to a stream of sub-editors, most of whom had been dragged off football subbing. PA had a world scoop and instead of a quiet Saturday afternoon I didn't get away from Farnborough until Monday night.

Pat might have mentioned that but for extraordinary good fortune he could have been among the casualties. At the Royal Air Force display at Farnborough two years previously the press tent was situated on Observation Hill, the actual spot where the engine ploughed into the crowd and caused the majority of casualties.

In the aftermath of the disaster, in a gesture of faith and as a tribute to Derry and Richards, another test pilot, Neville Duke, took off in his Hunter and he too broke the sound-barrier. And in the spirit of comradeship which binds these unique men, another comrade, John Cunningham, quietly took Eve Derry home.

The final word from Pat Gregory: 'Later I asked Bob Carrington what had made him ask me to cover that day. I just had a feeling something was going to happen, he said.'

The man who took off after Derry's fatal accident, Neville Duke, was chief test pilot of Hawker Aircraft, a company bearing the name of the legendary Australian pilot, Harry Hawker. Like Derry, Duke had been a fighter pilot during the Second World War. His love of the air stemmed from childhood days in Kent when Sir Alan Cobham's air circus and other barnstorming pilots would give rides to the local populace at five bob a head. He joined the RAF as a trainee pilot in 1940 and was posted to a Spitfire squadron at Biggin Hill in 1941. Later he was to serve with the Desert Air Force in Libya and Egypt before taking part in the Italian Campaign. In the desert he was posted missing twice in five days, each time returning to his squadron on foot. During the Italian Campaign he was nearly drowned when he baled out over a lake and was dragged under by the chute.

When he returned to England towards the end of 1944, he had a DSO, DFC and two bars and twenty-eight enemy aircraft to his name. He was still only twenty-two.

His next posting was on attachment to Hawker for production testing, a test pilot's course followed and then a posting to the Ministry of Supply Establishment at Boscombe Down, interrupted by a world-record attempt in an RAF team of Meteors. By now he was utterly engrossed in the world of high-speed flying and in 1948 he took the decision to leave the RAF and join Hawker as a test pilot. He became chief test pilot in 1951 on the death of Squadron-Leader 'Wimpy' Wade in an accident.

The year after the Farnborough disaster, Duke was awarded the Segrave Trophy for breaking two World Air Speed records in a Hawker Hunter Mark 1, with Rolls-Royce Avon RA7 engine.

The first was a speed of 727.6 m.p.h. over 1.8 miles at Littlehampton, Sussex, on 7 September and the second, 709.2 m.p.h. over a closed-circuit course from Dunsfold Aerodrome, Surrey, on 19 September.

The importance the government of the day attached to these achievements can be gauged by the fact that the formal presentation of the trophy at the RAC was made by the Secretary of State for Air, The Rt Hon. Lord de l'Isle and Dudley, VC.

Duke had one very lucky escape in the Hunter. The engine failed over Littlehampton. In his own words:

> I opened the throttle ... and nothing happened.
>
> I knew I didn't have enough height to reach base so I

> decided to set her down on Thorney Island. The plane kept bouncing so I decided to select 'undercarriage up'. I careered along the runway on the plane's belly and hurtled through a hedge, over a ditch and crashed headlong into the sea wall. The plane distintegrated around me and I broke my back. I was off four months.

Which for laconic understatement is hard to beat.

Such was the swift march of progress at this time that when in 1956, only four years later, Peter Twiss, DSC and bar was awarded the Segrave for breaking the World Air Speed record, it was at a fantastic speed of 1,132 m.p.h. The aircraft was a Fairey Delta II. The record eclipsed a valiant World Speedboat Hour record of 79.66 m.p.h. by Norman Buckley in *Miss Windermere III*.

Lionel Peter Twiss, educated at Sherborne, served in the Fleet Air Arm from 1939 and after the war became a test pilot. At the time he won the Segrave, he had flown 140 types of aircraft and, it was said, more high-performance planes than any other Englishman.

On 10 March 1956, Twiss took off in the Delta from Boscombe Down, the plane being powered by a single Rolls-Royce Avon jet engine. He made a flight in each direction over a 9-mile course between Chichester and Ford, Sussex. His first run was 1,117 m.p.h. and the return 1,147 m.p.h., giving an average of 1,132 m.p.h. and wresting the world record from the USA. The amazing thing was that Twiss had beaten the existing record by no less than 310 m.p.h. or rather more than 37 per cent. Posterity has not recorded what Colonel 'Dude' Haynes, the American in question, thought of it all.

The Segrave Trophy was presented to Peter Twiss at the RAC by the Minister of Supply, Mr Aubrey Jones, and at the time it was pointed out that Great Britain now held the world record on land, water and in the air.

Prince Philip sent his congratulations, a presumably grateful government gave Peter the OBE (which seems a bit niggardly since this is the sort of decoration they hand out to civil servants with the afternoon tea and biscuits) and Fairey Aviation promoted him to chief test pilot.

However, Twiss was getting a little disenchanted with the

world of aviation and in 1960 he quit, turning his attention to the water and becoming general manager of Hamble Marina in what was later to become TV's *Howard's Way* country.

There's little doubt that Peter Twiss was, and is, made of the stuff which triggered Hinkler and Kingsford-Smith to fly the world by the seat of their pants. The new world of boardroom politics, egghead technicians, smooth-talking accountants and pilots who were expected to be robots was not for him.

He confessed that a lot of the fun had gone out of flying. 'Flying in what I call the early days was much more individual and much more fun. You weren't in the hands of technicians.' He missed it for a while – which, after twenty years of solid achievement in aviation is not surprising – but was soon immersed in his new career.

However, it would be too much to expect that Peter could keep away from speed and he found a new outlet for his energies in powerboats.

This truly being a small world he took part in one Round Britain race with rally-driver Roger Clark, another Segrave winner, as co-driver. (Roger's comment: 'How did I let them talk me into it?')

In the year Peter Twiss quit as a test pilot, a 42-year-old who learned to fly at Brooklands before the Second World War, Lincolnshire-born Thomas William Brooke-Smith was awarded the Segrave Trophy. He had spent the war as a test pilot and was appointed chief test pilot to Shorts in 1948, being responsible for all experimental work. 'When work started on a direct-lift jet aircraft, the SC1, in 1954, I thought it would be a good aircraft to bow out on.' And so it was. The Segrave citation was 'for outstanding flight test work, culminating in 1960 in the transition from vertical to horizontal flight. The SC1 was the first British direct-lift jet aircraft to accomplish this feat, which is of the greatest importance to the future development of vertical take-off military and civil aircraft.'

Tom Brooke-Smith was as good as his word. When he climbed out of the cockpit on the Sunday of the year's Farnborough Air Show it marked the end of his active career as a test pilot. But flying was in his blood and he couldn't leave it altogether. So he formed his own company.

Lord Brabazon of Tara, vice-president of the RAC, England's first aviator (he held the No.1 certificate issued by the Royal Aero Club), First World War ace and one-time Minister of Transport, presented the trophy to Tom.

Brabazon was very much a man in the Segrave mould. Creator of the Cresta Bobsleigh Run, a racing motorist who won the Circuit des Ardennes and – in 1909 – winner of the *Daily Mail* £1,000 prize for flying a circular mile in an all-English-made machine.

At the presentation to Tom Brooke-Smith, this remarkable man commented.

> This new conception, the SC1, introduced new horrors for the test pilot. He had to rise from the ground due to the push on the part of the jet engines and, unlike rising from the ground in an autogyro, he knew that if the engines failed he must come down like a stone. Then there was the transition from vertical to horizontal flight. All this required great skill, great knowledge, great calmness and a very remarkable type of man. All these characteristics are embodied in Brooke-Smith. We saw at Farnborough a demonstration of this machine we shall never forget because it marked a big development period in the history of flight. This Trophy has had worthy past winners but nobody is more worthy of it than Tom Brooke-Smith.

Impressed as the Awarding Committee had been by this type of machine it was no surprise when, two years later, the trophy went to A.W. 'Bill' Bedford, OBE, AFC, AFRAeS, chief test pilot of Hawker Aircraft since 1956, for his development work on the Hawker VTOL (vertical take-off and landing aircraft).

Bedford had joined the RAF in 1940 at the age of twenty and stayed in the service until joining Hawker as an experimental test pilot in 1951.

His illustrious career was spangled with awards and decorations including the King's Commendation (1949), the Alston Memorial Medal (1959), the Davey-Richards Memorial Medal (1960) and in 1950 and 1951, the De Havilland Trophy (twice) and the Manio and Wakefield Trophies. In 1956 he had broken the London–Rome, Rome–London speed records and – more shades of Bert Hinkler – at one time held the British and United Kingdom gliding records of a distance of 257 miles and an altitude of 21,340 feet. He also had the Gliding International Gold 'C' with two diamonds.

A married man with two children, his hobbies in addition to gliding are squash, cricket and swimming.

During three years of development, mainly by Bill and his colleague Hugh Merewether, the swivel-jet Hawker did more than 1,700 take-offs and landings. It had flown forwards at faster-than-sound speeds, backwards at about 30 m.p.h. and even sideways at nearly 70 m.p.h. Like Tom Brooke-Smith, Bill Bedford received the Segrave Trophy from the hands of Lord Brabazon.

Supersonic airliners were the subject of much design and development work in the 1960s and when the Segrave Trophy was next awarded to a test pilot it would be for work on a new, fast, giant passenger craft.

The year was 1970 and the recipient was Brian Trubshaw, BAC's chief test pilot and the man who took the mighty Concorde up on its first flight in 1969.

At the time of the award, the British version of the Anglo-French project had completed 200 hours' flying-time and, for more than half that total, Brian Trubshaw had been at the controls. He had also flown the French version on a short trip.

At this time he lived at Weybridge but his work took him to Filton, near Bristol, and London, as well as the airfield at Weybridge (the old Brooklands motor-racing circuit). Sometimes he flew from place to place in his own two-engine plane, at other times he drove – in his Ford Zodiac.

Like those other test pilots who had won the Segrave Trophy Trubshaw had an illustrious record. He served in the RAF from 1942 to 1950 mostly with Bomber and Transport Commands although between 1946 and 1948 he was with the King's Flight, being awarded the sovereign's personal award for loyal service, the MVO. In 1964 he was awarded the MBE and in 1970 the CBE.

In 1961 and 1964 he was awarded the Derry-Richards Memorial Trophy and in the latter year he also received the Richard Hansford Burroughs Memorial Trophy (USA) and the R. P. Alston Memorial Trophy.

These awards were not all connected with Concorde for Trubshaw was also responsible for the development of the VC10, the Super VC10 and three versions of the BAC 111.

The memory of that first Concorde flight when he lifted 110 tons of Anglo-French technology into the sky for 22 minutes will always be with him: not least the delay of 48 hours occasioned by various hitches, notably a warning flag which appeared on the air-speed indicator each time he taxied down the runway.

Frustrating and irritating as it was, that 48-hour delay does not qualify for Brian's most hair-raising memory. That is a toss-up between the time when he was flying a twin-engined Beagle 206 at about 180 m.p.h., looked out of the window – and saw that there was no propeller on the right-hand side ('I called up Farnborough and said I wanted to do an imaginative landing fairly quickly'); and another occasion when he was flying the VC10 prototype. An elevator failure started a flutter, the plane began to vibrate violently and a lot of structural damage resulted. Then the right-hand engine gave trouble ...

'In the end I got the plane down but, yes, I felt fear.'

Not surprising since only three months before the BAC 111 prototype had crashed, killing all the crew.

HRH Prince William of Gloucester, a very keen flying enthusiast, presented the Segrave Trophy to Brian Trubshaw but, alas, in 1972, Prince William was himself killed when his plane crashed shortly after take-off near Wolverhampton while taking part in an air race.

'Trubby', as many of his friends knew him, was one test pilot whose story had a happy ending. A bachelor until he was forty-eight, he married in 1973.

As a small boy, the present writer watched air displays at Hendon Aerodrome. Not long before the war came the opportunity to get into the cockpit of a Hawker Hart two-seater fighter and handle the Lewis guns (which led me to a determination to be an air-gunner in the Second World War). The point, however, is that to folk in North London, Middlesex and Hertfordshire, Hendon meant the RAF. Bleriot, the pioneer aviator, once ran a flying school there, the Hendon air displays were major attractions and when war broke out in 1939, Hendon became a front-line station. In the summer of 1940 when waves of German fighters crossed the Channel, Hendon was in the thick of things.

So it was a sad day when in April 1987 the RAF ensign was lowered for the last time. Fittingly, it poured with rain and a planned Spitfire and Hurricane fly-past had to be cancelled.

Among the many wartime pilots who attended the last rites was one whose flying career had taken off at Hendon, who had had an illustrious war career and then became a famous test pilot, the last but not the least of the test pilots who, up to the present, have won the Segrave Trophy – Group Captain John 'Cat's Eyes' Cunningham, CBE, DSO, DFC, DL, whose distinguished career began with No. 604 County of Middlesex Squadron Auxiliary Air Force.

Far too good-natured a man to get belligerent about it, he is, nevertheless, none too keen on his nickname which was bestowed upon him during the war when he was our top night-fighting ace. The story was put about that John had the eyes of a cat and was so successful because he could see better in the dark than most human beings. This exceptional night-vision of his was said to be improved by eating plenty of carrots.

The stories certainly encouraged youngsters to eat plenty of carrots (there wasn't much else except Brussels sprouts, Spam and whale-meat in wartime) but were otherwise completely untrue.

Here is the truth of the matter from John himself.

> I did *not* eat carrots to improve my night vision. Carrots do provide a vitamin that helps people to benefit from whatever night-vision they were born with but they won't provide something which isn't there to start with. The propaganda people put it about that I ate carrots to explain why I had early night-fighter successful combats. The real reason for my success was, in fact, that my radio operator and I used some of the earliest radar equipment which was fitted into my Beaufighter. Of course, the authorities didn't want the Germans to find out too soon what we were doing, hence they invented the story about the carrots as a sort of smokescreen.

With the end of the war John became chief test pilot at De Havilland with full responsibility for test flying the world's first jet airliner, the Comet (not to be confused with the pre-war racer) which took to the air for the first time in 1949. During a long and illustrious career as a test pilot he was also to be associated with the Trident jet airliner, the Dove and Heron light transports and the HS 125 business jet, as well as developing a system for making automatic landings in the dark. No carrots this time.

In 1947 he broke the World Air Speed Record over a 100-km closed circuit with a speed of 496 m.p.h. in a Vampire during the Lympne (Kent) Air Races. In 1948 he set a World Altitude Record of 57,492 feet (18,133 km). (A fine record this: five years later Segrave contender, Wing-Commander W. F. Gibb, DSO, DFC, assistant chief test pilot of the Bristol Aeroplane Company, set the record at 63,368 feet (19,406 km) in an English Electric Canberra, a height of over 12 miles.)

In 1950 John flew the DH Comet, with its four Ghost gas-turbine engines, from London to Rome in 1 hr, 59 mins, 36 secs, an average speed of 447.24 m.p.h. Four days later, he flew the same aircraft from London to Copenhagen in 1 hr, 18 minutes, 6 secs, an average speed of 454 m.p.h.

In 1955, he made the first round-the-world flight in a jet – the Comet III – and also became the first to cross the Pacific in a jet (Fiji to Honolulu).

This latter flight earned him the US Harmon International Trophy which was presented to him at the White House the following year by President Eisenhower.

Then, in 1962, the Rolls-Royce Spey-engined Trident clipped more time off London to Rome, doing the trip in 1 hour, 37 mins.

John was also a superb aerobatic pilot and his display in a DH 108 was the highlight of the 1948 Farnborough Air Show.

Honours came thick and fast, deservedly so. The OBE, the RAeS Silver Medal for Aeronautics, the Royal Aero Club Gold Medal, the CBE and, finally, the Segrave Trophy in 1978.

In announcing the award, the committee pointed out that

the trophy was normally given for a single achievement, such as breaking a speed record, winning a championship or mounting a motorized expedition, but that, on this occasion, it was going to a man for a lifetime's achievement.

It marked John Cunningham's retirement as chief test pilot to British Aerospace after more than forty years devoted to aviation but one only has to look at his record to see that, during his long career, there were several instances where he might well have been awarded the trophy. (John did not retire entirely from aviation but remained an executive director of the Hatfield-Chester Division of British Aerospace.)

Anyone less like a daredevil pilot than the modest, quietly-spoken John it is hard to imagine. He regularly attends the Segrave presentations. Peter Twiss and Bill Bedford have often appeared at them and others come from time to time. All of these fine pilots are especially welcome since, as Lord Brabazon once said,

> I looked up *brave* in the dictionary the other day and found the definition *without fear*. I beg to differ very much. If you have no fear then automatically you are not brave. Those who deliberately take on something that they know is dangerous and yet do it are brave. Under that heading, in my opinion, comes the test pilot. No test pilot ever took up a new aeroplane into the sky without qualms of anxiety in his soul.
>
> They are very brave men ...

Part II
The Fast Ones

Land- and water-speed record-breakers have figured prominently in the Segrave Trophy story which is hardly surprising in view of De Hane's career. Men and women have followed in his tyre-tracks and, sadly, two at least have followed him to a date with destiny in the dark waters of the Lake District. Yet always others have been on hand to pick up the torch, to venture into the unknown and to go where no one has gone before. There will always be such people.

4 *Like Father Like Son*

Sons of famous fathers have a burden put upon them which the rest of us do not have to carry, a burden which becomes even heavier if they try to achieve success in the same field as their parent. Randolph Churchill, Winston's son, failed abysmally as a politician, and even as an author – and he was a good one – trailed behind the elder Churchill. Richard Hutton, Billy Sutcliffe and Chris Cowdrey had brief spells in representative cricket – but never came within a six-hit of emulating their illustrious dads – Leonard, Herbert and Colin.

John Barrymore was a theatrical and cinematic idol until the drink got to him, his Hamlet they said was one of the finest ever seen on Broadway, yet his son got lost in a welter of Hollywood B-movies.

There are exceptions, of course. Brian London followed his father in winning the British heavyweight championship and George Eastham followed his by becoming a soccer international. Without doubt, sons who try to emulate their fathers have a tough row to hoe and no one found it harder or had to endure more criticism than Donald Campbell when he set out to follow the road to fame his parent had taken.

The most successful World Land Speed record-breaker of all time (he broke the official record nine times between 1924 and 1935), Malcolm Campbell was the first man to exceed 300 m.p.h. on land. Two years later he established a World Water Speed Record which he eventually raised to 141 m.p.h.

His son, Donald, fired by the same ambitions, raised the water-speed record to 276 m.p.h., almost double that achieved by his father. On the day of his tragic death on Lake Coniston he had attained a speed in one direction of 297 m.p.h. A return speed of 303 m.p.h. would have broken the 300 m.p.h. barrier over water as his father had broken it on land.

My good friend, the late Tommy Wisdom, *bon viveur* and raconteur, journalist and racing and rally-driver, was not only a friend of both Malcolm and Donald Campbell but also an active participant in their record-breaking activities.

In Tommy's opinion, Grand Prix motor-racing required tremendous skill and knowledge combined with a refusal to be frightened. Record-breaking, on the other hand, involved the minimum of skill but did require maximum courage. Both Malcolm and Donald had this special kind of courage in Tommy's view.

Having said that, Tommy felt that in the end neither Malcolm nor Donald achieved what they wanted – the mysterious Grail they pursued was always just out of reach. The father gained both land- and water-speed records but he badly wanted the air-speed record too. By the time he had gathered the records on land and water, others had put the air record far beyond his reach.

Donald always wanted to emulate his father. At a Brooklands meeting they turned up dressed in similar fashion, both riding motor-cycles, both dressed in similar fashion. The effect was spoiled by the motor-bikes falling over after they had been carefully parked and in a way was symbolic of the stormy lives both father and son led.

Tommy saw as much of the dark side of Malcolm Campbell's nature as anyone save Campbell's family and his loyal henchman, Leo Villa. Yet most of his recollections of the man were happy ones ... a shared journey to the USA when Tommy wired back a story that the *Aquitania* was going around in circles after trouble with the rudder – and the captain censored it. Another time when Campbell's speed attempt at Daytona Beach was delayed because it was 'windy' and Mayor Armstrong of Daytona was told that Tommy's story in the London press said that Campbell was 'windy'. He cabled London demanding a retraction. London put him right, the mayor gave Tommy a case of Scotch and Malcolm and Tommy remained the best of friends.

In 1929 when Campbell's Bugatti burned out, a lad named

Basil Cardew, later the distinguished motoring correspondent of the *Daily Express*, had been sent to assist Laurie Cade in covering the races.

Cade dispatched Cardew to interview Malcolm Campbell on the disaster which had befallen him. He turned in a wonderful story – vivid descriptive writing which really put the reader in the place of the hapless Campbell as his car went up in flames and smoke. A little later Cade and Cardew were walking through the pit area when a driver in overalls lounging against the pit counter waved to Cade.

'Who's that?' queried the lad.

'You should know,' said his boss. 'That's Malcolm Campbell.'

Malcolm Campbell had his critics, yet he was first in line if an essential job had to be done. When war came in 1939, he tried with the aid of Tommy and Bill Mackenzie, of the *Daily Mail* (and later the *Daily Telegraph*) to form a Motor Cycle Corps. The scheme fell through but it was typical of the attitude of the man towards life's problems.

In some ways Donald the son was very different. He was intensely superstitious. His father may have been ('although if he was, I never realized it,' said Tommy) but Donald most certainly was. Stories that on the night before his death he drew the ace of spades – the 'Death Card' – in a card game, and that he was visibly affected, have been argued about in print but Tommy believed them.

He recalled an incident on the ill-fated 1960 land-speed record attempt. Donald was not an experienced car-driver like his father and an E-type Jaguar was brought down from Los Angeles, 750 miles away, so that he might gain experience of how to handle a fast car in a slide on the Salt Flats. When the Jag arrived it was found to be painted green. Donald, who firmly believed green to be an unlucky colour, refused to drive it. In this, perhaps, son was like father, bearing in mind the preference Malcolm had always shown for his cars and boats to be painted blue.

The night before the 1960 crash, Donald said he would like to change the foot accelerator on *Bluebird* for a hand-throttle similar to the one used on the speed-boats. Leo Villa and Tommy Wisdom dissuaded him. That decision may well have saved his life. When the crash came there could quite possibly have been an explosion had the hand-throttle been in operation keeping the engine at full revs. As it was, Donald's foot came off the conventional accelerator and the engine just kept ticking over – if you can say that a turbine just ticks over.

After the crash, doctors at the local hospital, accustomed to dealing with the 'hot-rodders' who were their frequent guests, thought that Donald could be 'back on the track in two days'. Tommy insisted that a specialist be called and one was flown in from Los Angeles. He diagnosed a fractured skull.

These then were incidents which dotted the recollection of one man as he talked about the days when he raced against and worked with Malcolm and Donald Campbell. The legacy they left the world, he felt, was courage.

'After all,' said Tommy, 'record-breaking on land or water is just like a game of Russian roulette and at any moment the loaded chamber may be the one aimed at your head.'

The Campbell story began on 11 March 1885, when Malcolm Campbell was born at Chislehurst, Kent. It ended on 4 January 1967 when Donald Campbell died on Coniston Water. The two of them achieved something never likely to be repeated – between them they won the Segrave Trophy six times.

From his early days Malcolm Campbell had, in his own words, an incurable thirst for speed, so much so that at Bromley Police Court he was charged with driving a bicycle to the danger of the public, having ridden at 27 m.p.h. to 'the confusion and terror of two elderly ladies'. The magistrate fined him thirty shillings and hoped 'that this will be a lesson to you not to travel so fast in future'. Little did he know.

The demon cyclist's competition career proper started with motor-cycle trials; after that he flirted with a brief and expensive aircraft venture, and then switched back to motor-cycles and then cars. He raced at Brooklands before the Great War and enjoyed some successes. At that time his cars were named *The Flapper* after a famous racehorse and it was not until a friend told Campbell of a play then running in London, Maurice Maeterlinck's *The Blue Bird* that Campbell adopted the name which all his cars and boats and his son's after him would bear. For some reason, the name so fascinated the young race-driver when he heard it that he knocked up the owner of a paint shop, dashed home and proceeded to paint blue the car he was to drive at Brooklands on the morrow.

The day before the Great War began, Campbell drove in the last race; the next day he set off for France as one of the RAC's volunteer squad of car drivers. Later he transferred to the infantry and, in 1915, to the Royal Flying Corps. Oddly enough, in view of his later exploits, he was reckoned to be too hamfisted to be a top fighter pilot and he spent most of the war ferrying planes across the Channel.

Returning from the war as a captain with an MBE, he found his insurance business still prospering to such an extent that he could devote much of his time to motor-racing and this he did apart from a couple of ill-fated ventures into the motor-trade. Trivial Pursuits players may like to know that at one time there was a car on the market known as the Gregoire-Campbell.

Brooklands reopened in 1920 and Campbell won the very first race in his pre-war 2.6-litre Talbot at a speed of 84.5 m.p.h. He also took a first stab at record-breaking and driving a 1912 7.6-litre Grand Prix Peugeot gained a number of class records at distances from half to ten miles, the half being covered at 100 m.p.h. Among the other competitors at Brooklands that year was one Henry Segrave.

At the beginning of the 1921 season Campbell in his Talbot finished second to Segrave in a 3-litre scratch race. Segrave was driving a prototype Sunbeam. Campbell continued to race – and frequently win – at Brooklands during the next three years but increasingly his thoughts turned to record-breaking.

The World Land Speed Record (an unofficial description for the fastest of the International Class records) had been broken in 1922 by Kenelm Lee Guinness in a Sunbeam. Campbell borrowed the car and on Saltburn Sands set a new record for the mile although it was just below KLG's (yes, the sparking plug was named after him) record for the kilometre. However, the runs had been hand-timed and the International Commission refused to ratify them.

The following year, Sunbeam having been persuaded to sell him the car, he went to the Danish Fanoe Island and promptly broke the record. This time the International Commission refused to ratify it because, although electrical timing equipment had been used, it was not of an approved type.

Lesser men might have turned to something else after such disappointment, especially when the record was captured by yet another Englishman, Ernest Eldridge. But Campbell was back at Fanoe in 1924 with a new streamlined body on the Sunbeam and Brooklands' clerk of the course and official timekeeper on hand with the RAC's approved timing equipment.

The beach was in poor condition and littered with debris from the sea. Worse still, spectators were allowed to crowd right up to the edge of the course. At 150 m.p.h. Campbell lost his front tyre which bounded into the crowd, killing a boy. The meeting was abandoned.

Campbell would not give up. On Pendine Sands, South Wales, in vile conditions, he took the world record for the first time narrowly beating Eldridge's figure, but he badly wanted to be the first man to 150 m.p.h. and so, in July 1925, he went to Pendine again and in better conditions achieved his target. At the time it was an achievement which caught the public' imagination rather as did Roger Bannister's four-minute mile in later years.

The next few years were to see some wonderful struggles for the record, the main protagonists being Campbell, Segrave, Parry Thomas, Kaye Don, the New Zealander 'Wizard' Smith and the American race-drivers, Ray Keech, Frank Lockhart and Lee Bible. Thomas, Lockhart and Bible lost their lives in attempting the record.

Segrave held the record at the time of his death but on 5 February 1931 Campbell recaptured it at Daytona, improved on it a year later and then the following year pushed it up to 253.97 m.p.h. The first of these successful bids earned him a knighthood just like Segrave before him, the third brought him the Segrave Trophy, the first car-driver to win it.

Nor was Campbell finished with the record. At Daytona in March 1935, he raised the figures to 276.82 m.p.h.

Daytona was nearing the end of its period in the limelight. The search was always on for better surfaces on which to attempt speed records and with South Africa having been tested and found wanting, attention turned to the salt flats of Utah in the USA. A freak of nature, the flats are in fact the bed of a large salt lake, covered in water during the winter months. In the summer under the fierce glare of the sun – 110 °F in the shade, if any shade can be found – the water evaporates leaving a salt desert (as any follower of TV's *Wagon Train* will know).

Attention was first focused on the flats through the efforts of a local driver Mormon David Abbot ('Ab') Jenkins, a native of Salt Lake City.

A tall, dark and handsome man who was preaching 'Don't drink and drive' in the 1920s and 1930s, Jenkins was one of the world's outstanding record-breakers and for a period of sixteen or seventeen years held records at almost every distance from the standing start 50 km to 10,000 km with the 50 miles, 100 miles and 24-hour records thrown in.

Jenkins, whose race-car transporter bore the legend 'Ab Jenkins, the World's Safest Driver', a claim he backed by saying that he covered 85,000 miles every year without accident, may not have been taken too seriously by the world's 'fast ones' in his road-safety efforts but they certainly took him seriously when he was record-breaking in his *Mormon Meteor*. Through the 1930s, the war years and the late 1940s and early 1950s, Jenkins was the chief adversary of British drivers such as Eyston, Cobb and Gardner.

Campbell was the first to follow him to the salt flats and in September 1935 at Bonneville, *Bluebird*'s driver became the first man to exceed 300 m.p.h., the official figure being 301.13 m.p.h.

With this landmark, Campbell decided to rest on his laurels in so far as the land-speed record was concerned. He had broken it no less than nine times and had been personally responsible for adding the last 70 m.p.h. to it.

He had been doing less and less racing, partly due to the absence of a competitive British Grand Prix car, but had plenty of other interests, all fiercely pursued although some of them were very fleeting: golf, photography, collecting china, breeding dogs and searching for buried treasure – he went on expeditions to seek silver in the Salvage Islands (it had been dug up a hundred years before he got there), pirate treasure in the Cocos Islands (someone had flogged fellow racing motorist Kenelm Lee Guinness some 'pirate' charts) and gold on the reefs off Africa (no luck). He was also motoring correspondent of the *Daily Mail* and *The Field* and an unsuccessful parliamentary candidate for Deptford.

None of these pursuits satisfied the man's thirst for speed so, like Segrave before him, he turned his attention to the water. Segrave's record had fallen to the American Gar Wood before Kaye Don, driving *Miss England III*, raised it to more than 100 m.p.h. For a time the record was a shuttlecock between *Miss England III* and a succession of *Miss America*s produced by the indefatigable Gar Wood. When Campbell decided to take a hand, Gar Wood held the record at 124.8 in *Miss America X*. *Bluebird I* was a wooden-hulled boat powered by the engine from Campbell's land record holder and in September 1937, at Lake Maggiore in Italy, he broke the water record for the first time with 128.3 m.p.h. and next day pushed it up a little to 129.5. A year later he went to Lake Hallwill, Geneva, Switzerland, and beat his own record with 130.94 m.p.h. during the International Speed Trials.

Campbell was far from satisfied and so *Bluebird II* was built with the same power plant but a revolutionary body designed by Reid Railton who was later to be responsible for a number of land-speed record cars. In August 1939 *Bluebird II* raised the record to 141.74 m.p.h. on Coniston Water and earned its pilot his second Segrave Trophy. With nine land records and four water records it cannot be said that Malcolm Campbell earned his Segrave Trophies lightly but then those were days when scores of brave men and women were breaking records in the air, on land and on water.

Two weeks after his new record the world was at war and Malcolm Campbell was back in the Army.

Six years later, Campbell, still holder of the World Water Speed Record, was back in Civvy Street and eager to carry on where he had left off, his immediate ambition being to use jet engines in *Bluebird* to raise the record to 200 m.p.h. and put it beyond reach of the Americans. The hull of *Bluebird II* was reconstructed at Portsmouth and De Havilland loaned a 4,000 hp Goblin jet engine. Trials at Coniston in the summer of 1947 were unsatisfactory, the boat swerving at speed and it was sent back to Portsmouth. Here it was decided to fit an underwater fin and after further trials in Poole Harbour the team went to Coniston again in August 1948. *Bluebird III* handled badly and the best it would do was 120 m.p.h.

It was the last and least successful of Campbell's record attempts. Sixty-two years of age he was already a sick man and the following year he was dead. It was sad that poor health and public criticism for the part he played in disposing of the popular Brooklands race track should cloud the final years of such an illustrious career.

Unlike many of his peers, Malcolm Campbell died in bed. But also unlike many of his peers he had a son to whom the torch could be handed.

The war had brought some disappointment to Donald Campbell, the RAF deciding that piloting a plane and a history of rheumatic fever were not a compatible combination. One can only guess at what went through his mind at that time although the present author, who had a similar experience, has a good idea. Anyway there was nothing to be done about it and Donald went on earning a living as an engineer.

At what period he seriously contemplated assuming his father's mantle as a record-breaker is also a matter of conjecture. It may well be that the thought was partly formed in childhood days when his father admonished him for taking his pedal-car to pieces but we have the word of Leo Villa, who as chief mechanic served the Campbells for forty-five years, that within a few weeks of Malcolm's death Donald had summoned him to say that he intended to 'start where the old Dad left off'.

It was a hard task he set himself: the ghost of a remarkable father; a complete lack of experience in racing either cars or boats; and the sniggers and sneers of those who either doubted his ability or thought he was cashing in on his father's fame.

Against that he had only his own determination and the loyal support and vast know-how of Villa. In the end it was to be enough but there were to be many shattering disappointments along the road.

The first was reminiscent of his father's earlier ventures. The team went to Coniston Water in 1949 but bad weather delayed a serious attempt for three weeks; then, with the boat flat out, Donald was blinded by a jet of oil. Just the same the news was broadcast to the world that he had broken his father's record and just as swiftly renounced with a statement that the timekeeping had been at fault.

In 1950 Donald tried again. This time the engine 'blew up' and while the team was waiting for a replacement they received the staggering news that an American, Stanley Sayers, had raised the figure to a devastating 160.32 m.p.h.

Back to the drawing-board with Donald's eternal optimism fuelled by an invitation to take part in the 1951 Oltranza Cup race on Lake Garda, a cup originally donated in memory of Sir Henry Segrave which several British pilots had tried to win. Win it Donald Campbell did – with Leo Villa, on his own admission, swearing and praying alternately as he hung on for dear life in the observer's seat. Lapping at nearly 100 m.p.h. *Bluebird* gained a well-deserved if frightening victory.

Anyone who thought that this fine victory was a good omen was in for more disappointments. *Bluebird* was shipped from Italy to Coniston for another record attempt but the days of summer slipped by with the boat not ready, the weather not right, the water too choppy, the engine running 'rough'. It was October and conditions were becoming wintry by the time the boat seemed to be nearing the right state.

Early one morning with the lake surface as smooth as looking glass, Campbell and Villa went out for a trial run. At 170 m.p.h. the boat spun into the air, threshed the water wildly like a harpooned whale in its death throes and began to sink. Campbell and Villa were fished out but *Bluebird* sank in 25 feet of water while being towed to shore.

When she was raised the reason for the disaster became clear. A submerged railway sleeper had torn a great hole in the bottom and the boat was wrecked beyond repair.

For Campbell it meant going back to making a living in the engineering industry.

But it was too much to expect him to keep away from record

attempts and within a year he was planning a new boat. Like his father, his first marriage had broken up and he had married again so it was a new beginning in more ways than one. The new boat was to have a metal hull and be jet-propelled. Three years were to elapse before it was ready to take to the water and, meanwhile, someone had moved the goalposts. Stanley Sayers had pushed the record up to 178 m.p.h. It meant, realistically, that the new *Bluebird* would have to clock in the region of 200 m.p.h.

On 23 July 1955 on Lake Ullswater, Campbell tried again. The day was overcast but dry and windless. Donald slipped into the cockpit, the cover was closed over him, the engines started up and *Bluebird* began building up speed over the 3½ mile run-up. By the time it hit the measured distance it was travelling at a terrific rate but looked as steady as a rock. Campbell turned and made the return run and knew, even before the official timekeeper appeared on the jetty, that he had triumphed at last. When the figures were given they were truly magnificent. The record had come back to Great Britain with a speed of 203.32 m.p.h. and Campbell had made his own little niche in history as the first man to travel at over 200 m.p.h. on water. The team was invited to the United States and on Lake Mead, Nevada, Campbell shattered his own record with 216.25 m.p.h.

He was awarded the Segrave Trophy, the third for the Campbell family. Leo Villa said: 'We were turning our back on six years of frustration and failure and a great wave of happiness broke over us.'

It also broke over *Bluebird*. So many sightseeing boats crowded around her on Lake Mead that their wash sank the world record-holder.

Campbell's triumph put paid to a trophy for several other outstanding competitors that year of 1955. Geoff Duke could have been in line for a second trophy having been World Motor Cycle Champion for the fifth successive year. Stirling Moss, who would in fact get it two years later, might have had it for becoming the first Englishman (with Denis Jenkinson) to win the Italian classic road race, the Mille Miglia.

And there was a most unusual contender. Richard Pape

drove an Austin A90, your ordinary family saloon, from the North Cape in the Arctic Circle to the South Cape in Africa, a distance of 17,500 miles, the first to have ever made the journey.

Campbell's success transcended all and, like swimming on a winter morn, once you've broken the ice there is nothing to it – much.

Having claimed the World Water Speed Record at last, Donald Campbell was to break it again and again.

In 1956 he raised the mark to nearly 226 m.p.h.; in 1957 to 209 m.p.h.; in 1958 to almost 249 m.p.h. The latter achievement earned him a second Segrave Trophy and Donald celebrated by setting a new record of more than 260 m.p.h. in 1959.

On 1 December 1959, broadcasting on the BBC Light Programme, I said:

> Thursday evening in London at the annual dinner of the Sports Writers Association, we shall be honouring Donald Campbell as one of our Sportsmen of the Year.
>
> It could hardly be a more appropriate time. In the past few weeks we've been given some glimpses of Campbell's plans to add the World Land Speed Record to the water record he already holds.
>
> In what has been termed a million-pound operation, a car weighing four tons and capable of 475 m.p.h. is being built and the first trials should take place next summer.
>
> The project is centred around a Bristol turbo-jet engine which means that if Campbell is successful his will be the first jet car to hold the world record.
>
> This is particularly interesting to me because I'm one of the few people who've had the privilege of driving in the first successful turbo-car, the Rover JET I.
>
> JET I is now in the South Kensington Science Museum so although you can go along to see it, I'm afraid you won't be able to drive in it. But perhaps I can give you some idea of what it's like.
>
> The cockpit is large and comfortable but it seems a bit ominous when they lock the doors. Apparently this is to prevent parting company with the car on the sharp corners of the test track. Switch on – and from the bulkhead behind the seats comes the high-pitched whine of a jet-plane. It rises to a

piercing scream, a horrible sound as if all the banshees of the underworld are howling after your blood.

The car moves off, picks up speed quickly. Your stomach seems to slide through your backbone – rather like a fast lift travelling horizontally instead of up and down. In no time at all the needle is up in the eighties and corners are taken at speed with hardly a squeal of protest from the tyres. A short straight and – presto – the speed rises to a hundred miles an hour. The wind whistles past. The scream of the engine fades away in the slipstream. The only sound is like the pebbles on a beach and the moan of the sea.

This indeed is jet-age motoring. No clutch, no gears. No warming-up to worry about. But ... is it the motoring of the future? Is the internal combustion engine going to give way to the gas turbine? No one yet knows. And opinions are sharply divided.

Fords in America have just completed their most successful gas-turbine project yet. Chryslers are forging ahead with a car which has done well running both on Diesel oil and on petrol. Rovers themselves have produced the T3 saloon, a rear-engined turbo car which represents a great improvement over the original JET I. Yet some remain unconvinced. As a top executive of one of Europe's most important manufacturers told me during the Motor Show, 'There is no future in turbo cars. The future lies with fuel injection.'

Maybe. Maybe not. But if Donald Campbell breaks the world record, the supporters of jet-age motoring will be flinging their hats into the air.

Good luck to him ... and goodnight to you.

Campbell's car was ready for an attack on John Cobb's land record during 1960 but on the Salt Flats of Utah it literally took off at 365 m.p.h., four tons of metal hurtling through the air for some two hundred yards. It bounced five times before sliding to a halt, a mass of crumpled wreckage. Miraculously, Campbell was alive and from his hospital bed he announced that as soon as he was fit again and the car could be rebuilt he would have another go. An effective answer to those 'behind the hand' merchants who said he lacked courage.

Sir Alfred Owen, the millionaire who had built the car, provided an appropriate comment. He said if the driver had the guts to try again he would rebuild the car.

The new *Bluebird* was a unique vehicle, the first car designed for a World Land Speed Record attempt to use a gas turbine engine. This engine, the Bristol Siddeley Proteus 755, would be described by engineers as a free turbine but more popularly as a turbo-prop. It drove all four wheels of *Bluebird* and, although no one realized it, this too made it unique, for only one other car was to take the record and have direct drive from engine to wheels. *Bluebird* and her like were to be superseded by true jets, relying entirely on their tremendous power for propulsion and having no direct drive. There was to be a tremendous fluttering in the official dovecots before such records would be recognized.

In March 1963 Campbell landed in Australia with the 30-feet-long *Bluebird*, his destination the Salt Flats of Lake Eyre in South Australia.

It had not rained at Lake Eyre for seven years yet hardly had the course been cleared than the rain came down in torrents. The course was prepared again – and it rained at Lake Eyre for the second time in seven years. The critics were in full cry although how any man could be expected to anticipate rain in a place which had had none for seven years is hard to imagine. Campbell flew to Western Australia in a vain bid to find an alternative site.

(In 1989, for only the third time in white man's history, Lake Eyre became an inland sea.)

Everywhere the wolves were at his heels. The kindest comments were to the effect that he had lost his nerve after the Utah crash. His difficulties were negligible according to his critics (most of whom were thousands of miles away at the time). Fleet Street had apparently 'nationalized' the undertaking off its own bat and decided that Campbell must be replaced as driver of *Bluebird*. Racing-drivers were interviewed and asked by people who had no say in the matter if they would be prepared to step into the cockpit when Campbell, either voluntarily or otherwise, vacated it. When Sir Alfred Owen was reported as saying that so far the project had cost £½ million pounds and there was nothing to show for it, Campbell snapped.

The team returned home with Donald issuing writs for slander against Sir Alfred, but the two men met and Sir Alfred terminated speculation with a laconic, 'We are going to work together again.'

In February 1964, Donald and his third wife, the cabaret star Tonia Bern, returned to Australia with the team. The weeks and months went by and in England Donald Campbell was almost a forgotten name. Then, on 17 July, *Bluebird* was wheeled out on to the lake-bed. There was a cross-wind blowing but Campbell decided to go. On his first run he was caught by the wind but straightened the car out and recorded 403.1 m.p.h. over the measured mile. On the return trip he recorded an identical time for a new world record. One of his tyres was right down to the fabric.

Unbelievably, the critics remained unimpressed. They seemed genuinely aggrieved that Donald had only broken Cobb's record by 9 m.p.h. One newspaper pointed out that a wartime Spitfire could do 450 m.p.h. although what that had to do with the Land Speed Record only they knew!

Campbell had another card to play. It was announced that before the year's end he would break his own Water Speed Record and no one, 'not even Donald's father', had broken both land and water records in the same year.

Lake Dumbleyung in Western Australia was chosen for the bid but again the weather was uncooperative. On the last day of December the waters calmed a little and Campbell went for the record. At 280 m.p.h. rough water buffeted the boat and over the radio Campbell cried, 'I've bought it, I've bought it, I'm going in.' But he straightened her out and streaked across the rippling surface to register 283.6 m.p.h. Two minutes later he was on the way back for his second run and the water was even rougher. Halfway on the approach for the second run his engine cut out. He restarted and decided to take a chance on a shorter run-up rather than go back to the start which would have meant refuelling. As he shot across the measured distance he yelled into the microphone, 'What's my speed?' and the answer came back '269'. He had beaten his own record by some 16 m.p.h. with a speed of 276.33 m.p.h., the first man to break both land and water speed records in the same year.

Tonia was so excited that she leaped into the water and swam out to her husband. Afterwards she said, 'People have been sneering at him and saying he is chicken. He has given them their answer.'

At such times Donald's father was never very far from his thoughts. As *Bluebird* was moored alongside a pontoon, he said, 'Boys, this is the eve of the old skipper's death sixteen years ago,' and the team and spectators stood in silence for a minute in memory of Sir Malcolm.

The Segrave Committee, meeting in London, had no doubts about their opinion of Donald Campbell's achievement and once again he was awarded the trophy. The nation, perhaps, was a little more grudging in its praise, his only official honour being the CBE.

On Thursday, 16 December Lord Camden presented the Segrave to Campbell and Segrave Medals to his team including the legendary Leo Villa. At a dinner later that evening Donald Campbell presented the RAC with a gauge from his *Bluebird* car. It showed the percentage power development by the Bristol Siddeley engine relative to linear acceleration.

Donald did not want to rest on his laurels but backers were not forthcoming for a new car and the old one had just about reached its limits in so far as the Land Speed Record was concerned.

When the uninsured car was wrecked by another driver during a demonstration run, Campbell's involvement in the Land Speed Record business was at an end.

There remained the *Bluebird* boat. It had been in store at Hounslow for twenty months since breaking the record, the hull was ten years old and the engine fifteen. The engine was the crux of the matter but Bristol-Siddeley agreed to replace the ancient ironware with an Orpheus jet (on loan) and with this Campbell felt that a bid to raise the Water Speed Record to 300 m.p.h. was on the cards.

On 4 January 1967, the turmoil of the waters subsided almost as quickly as it began. Soon only a breeze scuffed the surface and the boats, which worked systematically backwards and forwards, their occupants vainly scanning the depths for something, anything, which might give a faint flicker of hope.

For nine weeks, Donald and his team had been at Coniston awaiting a favourable moment, nine weeks of frustration, indecision, harassment and working and waiting. That morning the fateful decision had been taken and at about 8.50 a.m. Campbell started the mighty power unit of the fastest boat the world had ever seen, the 2½-ton *Bluebird*.

The silence was shattered as officials, mechanics, reporters and photographers, who had lived in a sort of twilight existence during the long weeks of waiting, suddenly realized, 'This is it.'

Campbell, tense and grim-faced, shrugged into the cockpit and the cover closed over his head. The giant craft nosed across the waters of the lake.

Campbell opened up. *Bluebird* lifted, accelerated, 100 to 150 to 200 to 250. As she flashed over the measured kilometre the official timekeeper radioed 'Plus 47'. That meant 297 m.p.h., 21 m.p.h. faster than Campbell's existing record and within easy reach of the magic 300.

At the south end of the lake which is nearly six miles long Campbell turned and headed back for the second run.

'Here we go,' his voice crackled faintly over the communications system. 'She's tramping slightly ... the water is not good ...'

Faster, faster, the boat hit the measured kilometre, accelerating all the time. Then, as the horrified watchers stood transfixed, 'She is going – I am on my back.' Like a dolphin rising from the surface of the sea, *Bluebird* soared nearly sixty feet into the air, somersaulted on to her back and, in a flurry of spume and spray, disappeared into the grim waters below.

Campbell had been 200 yards from his greatest triumph.

On 19 July 1967, Mrs Donald Campbell was presented with the Segrave Trophy posthumously awarded to her husband, 'for the inspiring example of courage, initiative and skill which he gave to his fellow countrymen, and on their behalf to the world, during his life and in the record attempt in which he met his death in January, 1967, and in recognition of his outstanding contribution in the fields of mechanical development and aerodynamics'.

The presentation was made at a ceremony in the Great Gallery of the Royal Automobile Club during which members of Donald Campbell's team were also honoured.

Gold medals were presented to K. W. and L. H. Norris, the *Bluebird* designers; Leo Villa, chief operational engineer; Maurice W. Parfitt and Anthony E. James, engineering and technical; and J. L. Stollery, hydrodynamics and aerodynamics. Framed copies of the citation went to Louis Goossens, in charge of radio communications and refuelling facilities; Kenneth Reaks, instruments; and Kenneth A. Pearson and Jack Lavis, engine specialists.

Later in the year Leo Villa was awarded an OBE.

What drove Donald Campbell? Villa hotly denied that he had a death wish as some suggested. Rather does it seem that he inherited his father's urge for speed and that he wanted to be a son of whom his father could be proud.

I never met the father. I used to see Donald from time to time in Pall Mall carrying bowler, umbrella and briefcase, in the days when he was seeking support for the fastest car yet; and, of course, when he was presented with his first three Segrave Trophies and on other occasions when a film of his unique double was shown at the RAC and when he presented the then chairman, Wilfrid Andrews, with an instrument from *Bluebird*. He laughed easily but there always seemed to me to be a terrific nervous tension there, the impression of a man living on a taut edge. Who can tell? But when BBC television reconstructed that final fatal attempt in Tony Haylam's *Across The Lake* that brilliant actor Anthony Hopkins seemed to me *to be* Campbell.

One newspaper suggested that Donald was an anachronism, 'trying to break records on an English lake when spacemen were circling the Earth'.

If Donald Campbell was an anachronism then perhaps the world could do with more of them. Because without men like the Campbells, father and son, precious little would ever be achieved.

And accusations of cowardice come poorly from men who do nothing more exciting in life than travel to the office in a suburban commuter train.

Malcolm and Donald Campbell have gone. Their deeds remain.

5 *On Four Wheels*

Three other World Land Speed Record-holders have won the Segrave Trophy – George Eyston, John Cobb and Richard Noble. Eyston won it in 1935, oddly enough not for the outright world record but for the 1-hour, 12-hour and 24-hour records. He was, indeed, the most prolific record-breaker of all time and is reckoned to have taken more international-class records than any other.

Despite a powerful athletic build he was not your *Boys' Own Paper* idea of a hero. Bespectacled and quietly spoken he was the *parfait gentil* knight – except that by some quite extraordinary lapse none of our monarchs saw fit to bestow a knighthood on him. He was an old man when I first met him – he was to die in 1979 aged eighty-two – but still intensely interested in cars, engineering and record-breaking and still a director of Castrol, the oil company founded by Lord Wakefield which was, and is, closely connected with all forms of motor sport and record-breaking. Some idea of what a remarkable man he was, even in his autumn years, can be given by the fact that he held a pilot's licence until he was seventy.

Like so many young men of his generation his first experience of the rough hard world was in the Great War. He served in France throughout, was wounded at Arras, won the Military Cross and was twice mentioned in dispatches. At one time he was ADC to General Wellesley.

After the Armistice, he resumed his study of engineering at Trinity College, Cambridge, where he was captain of the First Trinity Boat Club, and a good sculler. Subsequently, he established an engineering business in which his friend and partner was world record-breaking driver and Brooklands star, Ernest Eldridge.

He took up motor-racing himself after watching the French Grand Prix in 1921 and soon showed aptitude for the sport, winning the British Empire Trophy with his MG Magnette *Humbug*, which was painted in black-and-amber stripes just like the sweets. He won at Boulogne and La Baule, driving a Bugatti, and also won races in Czechoslovakia and South Africa as well as at Brooklands.

However, it was record-breaking which fascinated him most – one suspects that the engineering problems presented intrigued him – and he proceeded to set new marks in almost every type of car possible from long-duration runs in such unlikely machines as Singer and Riley Nine saloons to being the first driver to exceed 100 m.p.h. and do 100 miles in the hour in a 750 cc MG, records achieved at Montlhery, France, then as popular among record-breakers as Brooklands itself.

He captured the world 1-hour record at over 130 m.p.h. in the difficult-to-drive 8-litre Panhard-Levassor and with this and other cars held that particular record four times, the world 12-hour record three times and the 24- and 48-hour records twice each.

It was inevitable that a man who had just about all the worthwhile car records to his credit would not be content without a crack at the big one, the World Land Speed Record itself.

At the time, Malcolm Campbell held the record with a speed of over 300 m.p.h. but Eyston designed a car, *Thunderbolt*, especially for the job and in August 1937 he took it to the Bonneville Salt Flats in Utah for a crack at Campbell's figures.

He also took with him his international class record-breaker, *Speed of the Wind*, and while preparing *Thunderbolt* for the world-record attempt took time off to recapture the 12-hour record from the Americans despite atrocious weather conditions. The Rolls-Royce engined *Speed of the Wind* covered 1,964 miles in 12 hours, an average speed of 163.68 m.p.h.

It speaks volumes for Eyston's own spirit that he should accomplish this – most other drivers have found the world record quite enough to handle on its own.

There was bad weather, problems with the clutch, all the usual catalogue of major and minor disasters which always confront those who strive to go ever faster, but then in November *Thunderbolt* put the record up to 312 m.p.h.

It was then that Eyston's rival and friend, John Cobb, appeared with a revolutionary car. To stave off the challenge Eyston made modifications to lighten his car and went out again. In one direction he achieved 374 m.p.h. but travelling in the reverse direction found himself dazzled by the sun's reflection from the car's polished aluminium body. He promptly painted *Thunderbolt* black, drove back on to the flats and put the record up to 345.50 m.p.h. Two weeks later Cobb raised it to 350.2 m.p.h. but Eyston wasn't finished and next day went out and regained his title with 357.53 m.p.h.

Cobb went back to the flats in 1939 and on the eve of the Second World War took the record at 369.70 m.p.h.

The World Land Speed Record may not have been Eyston's most remarkable achievement for little could match the records he broke in the darkness of Montlhery when uncompleted track repairs had left a gaping hole in the banking. Few men would have carried on in such circumstances. Eyston's record-breaking also tended to obscure his undoubted ability as a racing-driver, one of his best performances being a class win at record speed with Count 'Johnny' Lurani co-driving his MG Magnette in the 1933 Mille Miglia road-race.

The French circuit at Linas-Montlhery, not far from Paris, was probably Eyston's favourite and indeed it was popular with many other record-breakers. In later years George would recall with pride the records he established despite that great hole in the track (George called it 'a chasm') and the nights when the tip of the banking was illuminated with electric light bulbs while Eyston's Hotchkiss broke the World 48-Hour Record. Shades of Edge and Napier and more primitive lighting in earlier days at Brooklands.

Another recollection gave him a great deal of amusement. In the middle of winter Eyston and some of his colleagues were sliding and slithering down a steep slope from the track to the roadway when a ferocious Alsatian came rushing out of an *estaminet* bent on attacking them. In George's own words, 'The dog struck the ice and went slithering on all fours out of sight down the incline.'

Despite the happy memories, Montlhery was also the track where he had his closest brush with death.

It was 1931 and in the 750 cc Magic Midget he was attempting to be the first man to cover more than a 100 miles in one hour in a baby car. He duly achieved this, covering 101.1 miles in the hour and taking the Class H International Record, but, being a very methodical man, he decided to do just one more lap to make sure that he had been going the full hour.

It could have been the most fateful decision of his life.

Jackson and Marney, two of his team, watched the car out of sight and then, suddenly, the exhaust-note cut-out and there was silence. They jumped into a car and tore off round the track. Eyston's car was rammed against an earthbank and burning fiercely. Braving the flames and the smoke they rushed to get the driver out, kicking in the side of the car to do so. No Eyston. He wasn't in the car. Although Marney was badly burnt, the pair searched around the wreck but to no avail – the driver had vanished.

It was a mystery to baffle Hercule Poirot. What in fact had happened was that the car caught fire while travelling at full speed. Eyston steered towards the in-field, managed to extricate himself from his seat in the tiny cockpit and threw himself out, with the car still doing 60 m.p.h. The driver of another car using the track stopped, lifted Eyston's 13 stone, put him in the car and drove to the nearest first-aid post. No wonder his colleagues couldn't find him.

Eyston was taken to hospital in Paris, badly burnt, but he was made of stern stuff and was back at Montlhery breaking records by December of the same year.

He made one concession to his accident. Thereafter he wore asbestos overalls, forerunner to the flameproof outfits Grand Prix drivers wear today.

The British Racing Drivers Club recognized his courage and his records with the award of their Gold Star.

Someone (I think it was Bill Boddy, long-time editor of *Motor Sport* and foremost authority on Brooklands) once asked George Eyston whether he felt sour that a knighthood had escaped him when Sir Henry Segrave and Sir Malcolm Campbell had been so rewarded?

'No,' he replied, 'I regard my *Légion d'honneur* as the equal ...'

There was a slightly melancholy postscript to the story of Eyston's records. At the outbreak of war, *Thunderbolt* was on an exhibition tour of New Zealand and so was marooned for the duration. Sadly in 1946 it was destroyed by fire. So perished one of the most remarkable of world-record-breaking machines – eight wheels, two Rolls-Royce aero engines with a total capacity of 73,164 cc, 30 feet long and weighing 7 tons.

Speed of the Wind has not survived either but the Eyston MG, EX 120, appeared at the June 1989 Silverstone meeting of the Vintage Sports Car Club, after a two-year restoration. It was later sold at auction for £60,000, a very modest price when one considers that an Alfa Romeo raced by Lord Howe went for £1½ million at the same auction.

Surrey-born fur-broker John Cobb, another big man, was like Eyston a Brooklands regular – as an enthusiastic youth he is said to have asked Malcolm Campbell for his autograph – who was to thrill the crowds with his exploits at the wheels of various giant cars including the 10½-litre V12 Delage in which Rene Thomas had broken the World Record in 1924.

Most of these hairy monsters required a big man to drive them, or at least a very strong man, especially on the not-too-smooth surface of the Weybridge track.

Cobb made his Brooklands debut on 11 July 1925, driving a 1910 F.I.A.T. and, harbinger of what was to come, won his race.

The great days were to come later. In 1933, he unveiled his Napier-Railton, powered by a 12-cylinder 23,970 cc Napier Lion aero engine which under the old RAC ratings was 145.5 hp, rather a contrast to the 7, 9 and 10 hp saloons popular at the time. (Anyone interested in the technical details will find a very full description in Bill Boddy's *The Story of Brooklands*.)

The new car, built in the Thomson & Taylor workshops at Brooklands, was designed for outer-circuit races at the Weybridge track and long-duration records (which would eventually lead to Montlhery and the Salt Flats of Utah). A primary objective was the World 24-Hour Record.

It was welcomed by enthusiasts at Brooklands since most of the old 'monsters' were no longer racing, an exception being Cobb's own Delage which Oliver Bertram drove. The car made its first competition appearance at the August meeting and straightaway broke the standing lap record at 120.59 m.p.h. and the Class A flying lap record at 137.20 m.p.h. Cobb followed up with a clutch of records at the track in October and November.

The following year when the Napier-Railton appeared at the Easter Meeting in mottled aluminium and green with black wheels it won the prize for the smartest car but that was only the icing on the cake.

Cobb went out to attack Sir Henry Birkin's lap record of 137.96 m.p.h. and, despite the windy conditions which made the giant car difficult to control, he clocked 139.71 m.p.h. Such was the pressure that the driver had to exert to hold the car on the banking that when he finished his fingers had to be gently eased from the steering wheel and his arms massaged.

In some races at the track, Cobb was beaten by the handicapper, his great machine always being the back-marker, giving a start to less powerful cars. But he climaxed 1934 by winning the Brooklands Championship Race at 131.53 m.p.h., beating Kaye Don's 1928 record by more than 3 m.p.h.

1935 was a great year for Cobb. At Bonneville in July he broke the 24-Hour Record at a speed of 134.85 m.p.h. and collected twenty other international class and world records. At Brooklands, he did the fastest ever lap of the track at 143.44 m.p.h. and the fastest speed ever recorded there – 152 m.p.h. He and co-driver Tim Rose-Richards won the 500 Mile Race there at 121.28 m.p.h. and, to put their achievement into perspective, this speed was not beaten in any other 500 mile race, Indianapolis included, until 1949 when the legendary American race was won at 121.33 m.p.h. – and this with a rolling start! Cobb collected a nasty cut on the face from a flying piece of concrete – and shared the BRDC Track Star with his co-driver and Oliver Bertram.

Cobb performed well at Brooklands in 1936 with his V-12

Sunbeam but the Napier-Railton was in business with a vengeance the following year when it won the BRDC '500' (actually 500 km not miles) at 127.05 m.p.h., Cobb crossing the finishing-line with an offside tyre flapping around the wheel, his daring earning him the Wakefield Trophy and £250, a not-inconsiderable sum of money in those days.

He also won the Broadcast Trophy and £100, his speed of 136.03 m.p.h. being the fastest speed at which a Brooklands race had ever been won.

There were lighter moments at the track, of course. One occurred when a film company was making *Death Drives Through*, a thriller in which the villain was played by a real-life Brooklands driver who was also a professional actor, Miles Mander. The film crew had constructed a realistic racing car from cardboard and set it up by the side of the track. Just then Cobb blasted by in the Napier-Railton and the car's powerful slipstream disintegrated the cardboard construction. One can imagine the looks on the film crews' faces.

The Second World War ended the Brooklands story to all intents and purposes but it always held a strong place in Cobb's affections. In 1948, in a foreword to Boddy's book, he wrote 'the name Brooklands will remain immortal as the cradle of the British Motor and Aircraft Industries'.

In view of the successes enjoyed by the Napier-Railton at Brooklands, Montlhery and, not least, the Bonneville Salt Flats, it was understandable that when Cobb turned his attention to the outright World Land Speed Record he went no further for a designer than the man who had created the Napier-Railton, Reid Railton.

An engineering graduate of Manchester University, Railton had made a close study of streamlining and had advised on the design of the various *Bluebirds* in which Sir Malcolm Campbell broke the record between 1931 and 1935. (Railton passenger cars were marketed from 1931 to 1939 but record-breakers always seemed to be the designer's first love.)

The car he now designed for Cobb was described at the time as 'the strangest piece of machinery ever constructed for human speed'.

Known as the Railton-Mobil Special, it had a detachable

aluminium skin which lifted off to enable the driver to get into his seat. The skin enclosed an S-shaped girder which did duty as a chassis, the two 1250 brake hp Napier aero engines (one drove the front wheels, one the rear) and the wheels themselves.

Thus the scene was set for a modern-day joust between the two Englishmen, Cobb and Eyston ...

Unlike most world-speed contenders at that time Cobb and Eyston had both had considerable experience of their venue so the epic struggle as the record passed back and forth was hardly a surprise.

Cobb had circulated the flats at terrific speed for 24 hours at a stretch; and when Eyston, at the wheel of *Speed of the Wind*, broke over thirty records in July 1936, he and his co-drivers roared round a ten-mile circuit for 48 hours and in 24 of them covered over 3,500 miles.

The deeds of Campbell and Segrave had dominated the story of the World Land Speed Record prior to the Second World War but the struggle between Eyston and Cobb must have equalled anything which took place before and after. Yet neither ever received full recognition from king and country. In fairness to all concerned, it may be that the shadow being cast over Europe by the aggression of Hitler and the Nazis, required so much attention that record-breaking across the Atlantic was but a side issue.

Like Amy Johnson and Jim Mollison, John Cobb served in the Air Transport Auxiliary during the war. Not only was his world record in cold storage, so to speak, but potential challengers from Germany (already on the Atlantic when war was declared) and Russia, plus a projected smaller car from Eyston, disappeared into limbo.

When war ended Cobb was determined not only to retain the record but to be the first man to beat 400 m.p.h. on land. On 16 September 1947 he *did* beat 400 one way but had to settle for a mean speed and a new record of 394.2 m.p.h.

To the fast ones there is always another challenge over the horizon. With the land record safe for the moment Cobb, like Segrave and Malcolm Campbell before him, turned his attention to the water-speed record with a striking-looking jet-craft, *Crusader*.

Alas, like Segrave before him and Donald Campbell later, Cobb met his death when on 29 September 1952, travelling at speed on Loch Ness, *Crusader* exploded.

Richard Noble came along much later in the story, being awarded the Segrave Trophy in 1983, after the World Land Speed Record had been in the possession of the American, Gary Gabelich, for some thirteen years.

One of the great merits of Noble's achievement was that he had even less experience of driving fast cars than Donald Campbell and, like Campbell, he had to knock on a hell of a lot of doors to raise the money for his record bid. And again like Campbell he was sniped at and sneered at by detractors for doing so. In a day and age when sponsorship is the name of the game in almost every activity, why anyone should pick on brave young men for seeking it only they know. Noble personally raised over £1½ million for his record attempt which ultimately had 11 sponsors and 214 contributing companies.

Before he set off on this dangerous exercise, Noble had never driven a car faster than 120 m.p.h. The fastest car he had ever owned was a Triumph TR6 and he had never competed in a motor race. The nearest he had come to any competitive motoring was an overland expedition to Capetown by Land Rover covering 35,000 miles in a year.

Yet, like most of those bitten by the record-breaking bug, Noble dates his own interest back to childhood when he saw John Cobb's *Crusader* on Loch Ness. After that, speed, cars, aircraft and aerodynamics became his absorbing interest.

Record-breaking might have remained a dream as it does for most youthful dare-devils. The necessity to earn a living – Noble worked for ICI and then GKN (Guest, Keen & Nettlefold) – marriage and a modest semi-detached in suburban Twickenham, it was the story of thousands of young men. With Noble, something snapped. He sold his car for £1,000 and built *Thrust 1* in garages at Thames Ditton and Chiswick, headquarters of the operation being home. *Thrust 1* had a short and colourful life, abruptly ended at RAF Fairford in 1977 when the car did a triple roll at around 140 m.p.h. The wreckage was sold to a scrapyard for £175 and with that modest sum Richard launched *Thrust II*.

The Ministry of Defence sold him an Avon 210 jet engine from a Lightning F1 and Richard took a stand at Motorfair to enlist support. The stand cost £6,000 but was worth it – 35,000 people visited in eleven days. It was probably this that brought most criticism. For a would-be record-breaker to set up his stall in the market-place was not 'the done thing, old boy', an attitude which would have been more understandable in Victorian times than today.

The path ahead was still a rocky one: at one time the engine was housed in the garage of Noble's home and the car's designer, John Ackroyd, worked in a derelict house which they rented for £5 per week. Money was so short that on one occasion they could not raise the price of a rail ticket to Birmingham so that John could see the space frame being built.

Noble drove *Thrust II* at RAF Greenham Common – without hindrance from Bruce Kent and CND – and gained six national speed records, including the mile at 248.87 m.p.h. The runway was only 10,000 feet long which meant that Richard was coming out of the measured mile at around 260 m.p.h. with only a quarter-mile in which to stop.

It was a long way short of Gary Gabelich's world record of 622.407 m.p.h. but it was enough to encourage more support and in addition the Ministry of Defence made available an Avon 302 engine which gave 19 per cent more power.

In 1981 the team went to Bonneville and before the rains came Noble had touched 500 m.p.h. and set a new fastest British driver and car figure of 418.118 m.p.h.

Back home the car was damaged when Richard overdid it at Greenham Common and had to put it sideways at 195 m.p.h. to avoid smashing it up. The car was rebuilt in nine weeks and then it was back to Bonneville, but this time it was already raining and they couldn't even get the car off the transporter. They refused to be beaten and moved to the Black Rock Desert in Nevada where in only three weeks they surveyed 120 square miles of desert and cleaned the course of every little piece of stone. This time Richard set a new British record of 590.551 m.p.h. The critics still had the whole exercise marked down as a failure but Noble knew he had touched 615 m.p.h. at one stage and was confident that next time he would break Gabelich's record.

The Short SC1, first British direct-lift aircraft, in flight, with Segrave Trophy winner Tom Brooke-Smith at the controls

A.W. 'Bill' Bedford, Chief Test Pilot of Hawker Aircraft and 1962 Segrave Trophy winner

The Hawker VTO (vertical take-off and landing aircraft) in which Bill Bedford won the 1962 Segrave Trophy

John Cunningham with the Segrave plaque and trophy

Malcolm Campbell loses a tyre in an early record attempt on the Pendine Sands

Working on the Sunbeam with which Malcolm Campbell broke the World Land Speed Record at Pendine Sands in 1924. Note Campbell's natty plus-fours!

Donald Campbell at speed in *Bluebird*

Fifteen-year-old Donald Campbell congratulates his father on being the first man to drive at more than 300 m.p.h.

A big man in a big car. John Cobb after breaking the Brooklands lap record in his Napier-Railton at a speed of 139.71 m.p.h. in 1934

A dramatic photographic sequence shows John Cobb's *Crusader* exploding on Loch Ness. Afterwards just a few pieces of wreckage floated on the surface

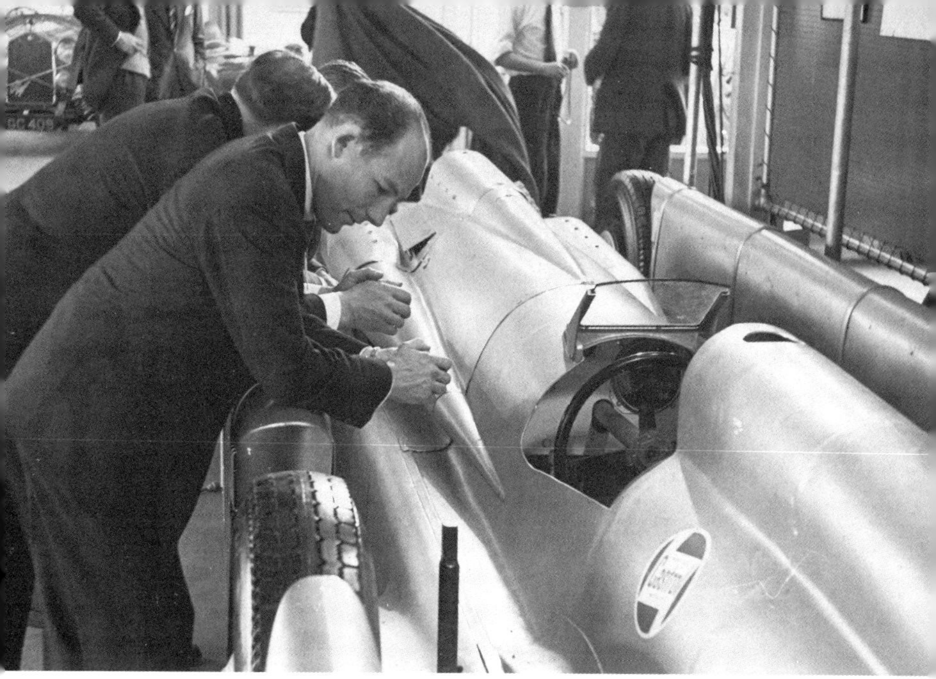

Stirling Moss, in reflective mood, studies Segrave's Golden Arrow at the National Motor Museum

Stirling Moss as the fans like to remember him – at the wheel of a Maserati

Captain G.E.T. Eyston in his International Class record-breaker, Speed of the Wind

When Richard Noble received the Segrave Trophy, a joke presentation was made to one of his team, Ron Benton. Noble may have been the fastest man on earth, but Benton, claimed his colleagues, was the fastest man on a toilet

And so it proved. On 4 October 1983, at Black Rock, Richard Noble took the World Land Speed Record at 633.468 m.p.h.

Gabelich himself was there to see his record broken and even showed Noble plans of a new *Blue Fame* with which he intended to regain the record if he could get the necessary backing. This was not to be. The following January the American was killed when his motor-cycle was in collision with a lorry in Los Angeles.

Noble was awarded the Segrave Trophy and designer Ackroyd the Segrave Medal. My own feeling was that Richard's charming wife deserved a medal too, not to mention the others of the eleven-man team who had sweated blood for no reward other than the satisfaction of achievement.

It was one of the happiest and carefree Segrave presentations ever with the tall (6 ft 1 in), dark 37-year-old Noble enjoying every minute of it and his team like a bunch of schoolboys on the last day of term. There was even a joke presentation when Ron Benson, the man responsible for the car's structure, was given a model 'loo' for reasons best left buried in the Nevada desert. Something to do with the fastest toilet in the West!

In November the British Racing Drivers Club presented Noble with a special Gold Star and honorary membership of the Club, a fitting tribute since the first Gold Stars went to Sir Henry Segrave and Malcolm Campbell and others later to John Cobb and George Eyston. Then, in January, the RAC announced that its Diamond Jubilee Trophy, which had been awarded only five times since its inception in 1957, was to go to Noble.

A postscript to the Richard Noble story: on the Jumbo jet which brought the team home from Nevada, the American captain told his passengers that Richard and co. were aboard, then said, 'We are now cruising at 570 m.p.h. – and if we were on the ground Richard would be passing us.'

It is not likely to be the final word in the Noble story. As this is written plans are afoot to attempt the fastest crossing of the Atlantic without refuelling in a 164-ft boat powered with a Rolls-Royce RB-211 engine. *Atlantic Sprinter* is to hold 83,760 gallons of fuel and would take 7½ days to fill up at an ordinary petrol station.

There was another outstanding British record-breaker in the 1930s in addition to Campbell, Eyston and Cobb, yet presumably because he never held the Land Speed Record his name has not gone down to posterity to the same extent. Lt Col. A. T. G. Gardner, known to one and all as Goldie, did in fact set some of the most fantastic records in the history of motoring and was a truly remarkable character.

Many folk, present writer included, thought Goldie was some sort of nickname, whereas it was his Scottish mother's maiden name.

Born in Essex, educated at Uppingham, Gardner left England at the age of twenty for forestry work in Ceylon, taking with him his motorcycle. On the island he first drove a car and also became a brilliant polo player. His next assignment was a five-year contract in North Burma but in April 1914 he contracted typhoid and malaria and was sent home on six months' sick leave during which he went around Brooklands for the first time – on a two-wheeler. He didn't return to Burma. The Great War broke out and he joined the cavalry as a second-lieutenant, later transferring to the Royal Artillery and becoming the youngest major in the British forces. He was mentioned in dispatches in 1915 and awarded the Military Cross the following year.

In August 1917 a reconnaissance plane in which he was flying was brought down near the enemy lines. Badly wounded, he crawled back across No Man's Land to his own lines. His right leg and hip were so badly injured that he would spend two years in hospital and endure twenty operations before being discharged from the Army in 1921 as unfit for further service.

It was unlikely material for a racing motorist and record-breaker but like Segrave before him, Gardner was made of stern stuff. He won his first Brooklands race in 1928 and enjoyed further successes in the next few years; he also won at Boulogne and competed in the 1929 and 1930 Irish Grands Prix and in the BRDC 500, but his career nearly came to a dramatic end during the 1932 TT race at Belfast. His MG somersaulted three times. The first time the mechanic was thrown out, escaping with very bad bruising. On the second Gardner was thrown out but unfortunately the car came down on top of him eventually coming to rest right way up but very much a wreck.

Gardner suffered a double compound fracture of his war-damaged leg and unfortunately it turned septic. Amputation was likely but the medics managed to save it and after four months in an Irish hospital he was back at his beloved Brooklands, walking with the aid of a stick. In 1934 he returned to racing.

What changed the whole course of his career was a trip to Daytona in March 1935 with his chum Malcolm Campbell. When Campbell raised his own record to 276.82 m.p.h. it whetted Gardner's appetite for record-breaking.

In 1936 he began. First there was an excursion to Daytona again, this time to compete in a stock car race. Back at Brooklands he won the Locke King Trophy at an average speed of 114.27 m.p.h., his fastest lap being an incredible 122.07 m.p.h., and this finally convinced him that there was a future in attempting records.

His first target was the British One Hour Record and, although he failed, he did establish a Class G 1100 cc Outer Circuit Record that was never beaten – 124.40 m.p.h.

In June 1937 he set an International Class G Record for the Flying Mile of 148.5 m.p.h. on the Frankfurt–Darmstadt autobahn and at Montlhery he set further Flying Mile and Kilometre records but back on the autobahn engine problems prevented him reaching his 150 m.p.h. target.

He now determined to achieve 200 m.p.h. but needed a new car for the job. The *Gardner Special*, as it was later named, was built in 1938 with the backing of Lord Nuffield and, basically, was an 1100 cc MG, beautifully streamlined by Reid Railton and built on the chassis of George Eyston's *Magic Magnette*, Ex 135, with which Eyston had won the British Empire Trophy in 1934.

In November the equipe were back at the Frankfurt autobahn and on the 9th Gardner recorded 186.6 m.p.h. for the Flying Kilometre and 196.5 m.p.h. for the Flying Mile, amazing figures for a car of that size and such a striking performance that he was awarded the Segrave Trophy, the committee taking into account the fact that he was 'improving the breed' of small cars, the cars that most people used on the roads.

Satisfying though his achievement had been, Goldie was still conscious of the fact that he had not exceeded the magic 200 m.p.h. so next May the team was back in Germany, this time at the newly constructed Dessau autobahn. On his birthday, 31 May, and despite a strong cross-wind, the little MG clocked 203.5 m.p.h. over the kilometre, 203.2 m.p.h. over the mile and 197.5 m.p.h. over 5 km.

For once the headlines told the story, 'Over 200 m.p.h. in a small car.' Because that was indeed the nub of the matter. An 1100 cc engine was approximately what was more often referred to in those days as a 10 hp engine and 10 hp engines were used to power small family saloons.

Not only had Gardner broken the 1100 cc records, he had also beaten the records for the next two classes, up to 1500 cc and up to 2000 cc.

So that night while the gallant soldier was in Berlin broadcasting to the BBC, his team overbored the engine to raise the capacity to 1,105 cc, making it eligible for the next class, Class F, and two days later Gardner pushed the Class F records up to 203.9 m.p.h. for the mile and 204.2 m.p.h. for the kilometre. He thus became the first man to exceed 200 m.p.h. in both Class G and Class F. If he had not won the Segrave in 1938 the committee would surely have had to give it to him in 1939.

Onward ever onward ... the next plan was Class H records, 750 cc, and arrangements were made to return to Dessau in October 1939. But Hitler had other ideas ...

During the war he served first in the Mobile Special Constabulary and later overseas with the Military Government staff at Montgomery's headquarters but as soon as peace broke out the 6 ft 3 in 'limping Major' as some of the press corps described him was back on the record trail.

Between 1946 and 1950 he smashed records in five further international classes, each – with one exception – being with variants of the original MG Magnette engine. On 31 October 1946 he took Class H (500 to 750 cc) records, his highest one-way speed being 164.72 m.p.h.; this with an engine the same size as a Baby Austin. In 1947 Class I fell; in 1948 Class E (1500 to 2000); in 1949 Class I again (the Italian Grand Prix and sports-car driver Piero Taruffi having temporarily snatched them away); and in 1950 Class J (up to 350). A four-cylinder XK100 Jaguar engine had been installed for the Class E records but for the smaller classes the Magnette engine was relieved of two, three and four cylinders very successfully, a complete turnabout from the usual process of *increasing* power.

Gardner, now sixty, was awarded the OBE, which many thought was poor official recognition of his efforts and of those of his faithful backroom boys, Syd Enever, 'Jacko' Jackson and others. Undeterred the veteran took off for the States and, partnered by Alan Hess, one-time Austin and later Simms Motor Units PRO, collected 48 national and US Stockcar Records at Eastport, Long Island, driving a standard A40 Devon saloon.

Further Class J records in Belgium were next on the agenda and then in 1951 and 1952 Gardner took the now well-trodden path to Utah and a further eight records, among them one he had set his heart on, the Class F One Hour Record. It was the end of the road for a man who had done much for his country and his country's motor manufacturers.

He was afflicted by a cerebral haemorrhage – his father had been killed by one – and he retired to Eastbourne, dying after five years of becoming progressively more helpless, something hard to take for such a dynamic man of action.

His record was his memorial: 35 International Class Records, 81 other speed records; winner of the Segrave Trophy; three times winner of the BRDC Gold Star; and the first non-Belgian to be awarded that country's medal for Sporting Merit.

The three decades in which he bestrode the record-breaking scene were also great years for MG cars – in record-breaking, in track and road racing and in the sales room.

The sad end to Goldie Gardner's career would not end the MG story. For the best part of another decade, MGs would be taking class records in the hands of drivers such as Eyston, Miles, Lockett, Wisdom, Ash, Ehrman, Leavens and Phil Hill. In 1954, for example, Eyston and Ken Miles broke 8

International Class F records and 29 national ones. And another Segrave Trophy was to be won by a record-breaking MG.

Only a handful of Grand Prix racing-drivers have won the Segrave Trophy and only one of them, Jackie Stewart, for his Grand Prix racing exploits alone, a fact which surprised him when I drew it to his attention recently.

In 1957 Stirling Moss was awarded the trophy on the strength of his Grand Prix achievements coupled with his record-breaking, the only time this has happened.

That year, Moss, driving a Vanwall, won the Grand Prix of Europe (British Grand Prix) at 86.80 m.p.h.; the Grand Prix of Italy at 120.28 m.p.h.; and the Grand Prix of Pescara at 95.55 m.p.h., the variation in speeds giving some idea of the relative trickery of the circuits. In addition, driving an MG, he broke five International Class F (1500 cc) records on the Salt Flats of Utah, the fastest being at 245.64 m.p.h.

Londoner Moss is an incredible character. By most counts the greatest driver never to win the World Championship he is a household name and years after his Grand Prix career finished – a career cruelly terminated by a major crash at Goodwood – he is the man of whom the British public in general think when racing-drivers are mentioned.

The time-worn query to a motorist stopped for speeding is still, 'Who do you think you are, Stirling Moss?' Mark you, on the odd occasion, a policeman has uttered the immortal phrase only to get the truthful reply, 'Yes, I am.'

He is a highly intelligent, thrusting, forceful personality and not the easiest person in the world to get to know, in contrast to his rally-winning, showjumping sister Pat, now very happily married to the genial Swedish rally ace, Saab's Erik Carlsson.

Stirling and Pat had the breeding. Father Alfred, a dentist by profession, was a good enough racing-driver to appear twice in the Indianapolis 500 without disgracing himself, while mother Aileen was a very good rally driver who used to frighten the pants off many a male driver by the speed at which she drove.

Beginning in 1948, Stirling first made his name in

Half-Litre or 500 cc racing which played a major role in reviving motor sport in Great Britain after the Second World War. Later he drove for the HWM works team, a brave effort by John Heath and George Abecassis to put Britain on the map.

Stirling was always eager to drive British cars if possible and often turned down tempting foreign offers but in the absence of a competitive home-grown Grand Prix machine was virtually forced to drive for the Italian Maseratis and the German Mercedes just as Malcolm Campbell, Lord Howe, Dick Seaman and others had to 'go foreign' pre-war.

But the situation was about to change. At Silverstone in 1956 he won the *Daily Express* Trophy in a British Vanwall and in 1957 joined the Vanwall team. Vanwall had been created by the ball-bearing manufacturer, Tony Vandervell, who started with a Vanwall Thinline Special, based upon a Ferrari, and went on to build one of the most successful of British Grand Prix teams.

At the time race enthusiasts in the UK had had little to cheer about apart from some gallant efforts by HWM and Connaught and the valiant deeds of Cooper in 500 cc racing. Tony Vandervell was to change all that.

At Monaco, Tony Brooks, another dentist, winner of the non-Championship Syracuse GP in a Connaught, took his Vanwall into second place behind World Champion Juan Fangio in a Maserati. At Rheims, Stuart Lewis-Evans in only his second Vanwall drive had shown up well, although Fangio was again the winner.

So the Grand Prix circus came to Aintree, Liverpool, where the British Grand Prix had been given the courtesy title of Grand Prix of Europe and it is arguable that there has never been a finer collection of drivers in one race. Juan Manuel Fangio led the Maserati team, backed up by the Frenchman, Jean Behra, the dashing Franco-American, Harry Schell and a new Argentinian talent, Carlos Menditeguy. Scuderia Ferrari, using Lancia V8s, lined up with two outstanding Englishmen, Mike Hawthorn and Peter Collins (England had better drivers than cars at the time), Italy's own Luigi Musso and the skilful and experienced Frenchman, Maurice Trintignant. There were three Coopers (Jack Brabham, Roy

Salvadori and Bob Gerard), two BRMs (British Racing Motor racing-cars) (Les Leston and Jack Fairman) and a couple of private Maseratis (Ivor Bueb and the Swede Joachim Bonnier). But the team on which much attention was focused was the all-British Vanwall line-up of Stirling Moss, Tony Brooks and Stuart Lewis-Evans.

They did not disappoint in practice and when the starting grid was finalized Moss was in pole position and Brooks was also on the front row with Behra (Maserati) between them. Fangio, the World Champion, unusually for him, was relegated to the second row, alongside Hawthorn, and Lewis-Evans in the third Vanwall was in the third row with Schell and Collins.

When the race began Moss shot into the lead, hotly chased by Behra. Hawthorn passed Brooks and the latter settled down to be 'towed' round comfortably in fourth place. At 10 laps Moss was leading Behra by over 7 seconds, at 20 he had increased his lead to 9 seconds but when Stirling passed the grandstands on Lap 21 there was a stuttering noise from the exhaust and the Frenchman had clipped 1½ seconds off Moss's lead.

Next lap Moss came into the pits and after rapid surgery resumed the race but something definitely ailed the car and he was soon back in the pits. Brooks was called in on Lap 26 and Moss took over his team-mate's car, resuming the race in ninth place.

Schell's Maserati boiled and bubbled into the pits. Moss was eighth.

Moss overtook Menditeguy. Seventh.

Lap 35 and he caught and passed the great Fangio. Sixth.

Lap 40 and he passed Musso. Fifth.

Now there were just Behra, Collins, Lewis-Evans and Hawthorn ahead of him.

At halfway (Lap 45) Behra was 9 seconds ahead of Hawthorn who in turn was 20 seconds in front of Lewis-Evans. Collins was a further 21 seconds back in fourth place and his Lancia sounded off-song. Moss was gaining on him rapidly and on Lap 47 he passed him.

Behra was equalling the lap record but Moss was breaking it. The French ace kept his nerve and on Lap 69 was 22 seconds ahead of Hawthorn, who was having a hard job fending off the two Vanwalls.

Then drama. The clutch and flywheel assembly of Behra's car broke and, as Hawthorn, Lewis-Evans and Moss roared past, Hawthorn punctured a tyre on debris.

With Musso the best part of a lap behind, the two Vanwalls eased off but on Lap 73 Lewis-Evans had trouble and eventually struggled into the pits, resuming the race in seventh place.

When Moss accelerated out of Tatts Corner for the last time and took the chequered flag, the crowd went wild, flooding on to the track. It was the first time a British driver in a British car had won the British Grand Prix and it was the harbinger of great days to come.

The final result of this historic race was:

1 Stirling Moss/Tony Brooks (Vanwall)
2 Luigi Musso (Lancia-Ferrari)
3 Mike Hawthorn (Lancia-Ferrari)
4 Maurice Trintignant (Lancia-Ferrari)
5 Roy Salvadori (Cooper-Climax)
6 Bob Gerard (Cooper-Bristol)
7 Stuart Lewis-Evans (Vanwall)
8 Ivor Bueb (Maserati)

Moss was to end the season runner-up to Fangio for the World Championship for the third time in succession.

In August, Moss took time out from racing for a spot of record-breaking, unusual to say the least. The target was an International Class record which had stood for eighteen years, Goldie Gardner's Class F (1500 cc) mark of 204.2 m.p.h.

Now MG had decided that they wanted to put the record up to 250 m.p.h. or at least 240 m.p.h. – four miles a minute. Moss was chosen as the driver and the car, built by MG guru Syd Enever, was the EX 181, described as 'a ground missile of the most advanced type' with the engine in the middle and the driver sitting well forward, rather like the German Auto-Unions of pre-war days or the Grand Prix cars yet to come.

There was the usual frustrating wait for the right conditions on the Utah Salt Flats but on the evening of 23 August 1957, Moss climbed into EX 181 and proceeded to break five Class F records, his highest average speed being 245.64 m.p.h. not quite the magic 250 but well over the desired 240. It was a personal record for Stirling too – he had just driven some 50 m.p.h. faster than he had ever done up to that time.

Thus, with that unusual combination of Grand Prix racing and record-breaking in the same season, Moss was awarded the Segrave Trophy. He still frequently attends the presentations today, restless, energetic and keenly interested in the exploits of others of that rare band of Segrave winners.

Another Grand Prix driver to be awarded the Segrave Trophy but *not* for Grand Prix racing was Bruce Leslie McLaren.

I first met Bruce McLaren over lunch at the Royal Automobile Club and found it hard to believe that this quiet, unassuming, baby-faced lad (because he was not much more) was the daredevil Grand Prix driver who had joined Jack Brabham in the Cooper team and was rapidly making them a force to be reckoned with on the race circuits of the world.

Bruce was one of a bunch of New Zealanders who made their mark in motor-racing through the 1950s, 1960s and 1970s – Denis Hulme and Chris Amon (who shared a winning drive with Bruce at Le Mans) were among the others – and he had shown he was good right from the beginning. On 12 December 1959 he became the youngest-ever winner of a Grand Prix when he won the United States race at Sebring, Florida. He was twenty-two. That year he also won the New Zealand Championship.

Behind the quiet exterior – he spoke but little but was always smiling – McLaren was an intelligent and ambitious man. When Brabham left the Cooper team to manufacture cars under his own name, Cooper moved McLaren into the No. 1 driver seat but Bruce too wanted to build and race his own cars.

The first McLaren car saw the light of day in 1964 and was an Oldsmobile-engined sports car designed primarily for the rich American races that eventually formed the basis of the

CanAm series which began two years later. Before that happened McLaren would also produce their first Grand Prix cars.

However, it was for his CanAm achievements that Bruce would win the Segrave Trophy.

From 1967 to 1970, Group Seven McLarens won the CanAm series four times in a row, Bruce himself being champion in 1967 and again in 1969 when he won *every* race in the Series. It was a remarkable feat made even more so by the fact that he not only drove the cars but designed and built them into the bargain. It rattled the Americans and no mistake – especially since, when Bruce didn't win, his team-mate, Denny Hulme, did!

Alas, before the Segrave Trophy could be handed over to Bruce he was killed while testing a CanAm McLaren at Goodwood. For the only time in history the subsequent Segrave presentation did not take place at the RAC. Instead, on the eve of the RAC British Grand Prix at Brands Hatch, the trophy was presented to Mrs McLaren, like Bruce New Zealand-born, in the Club House at the Kent circuit.

The object in switching to Brands Hatch was achieved because so many of Bruce's friends were able to be there – Denny Hulme, Chris Amon, Jack Brabham, Graham Hill, Jackie Oliver, Jochen Rindt, Dan Gurney, Pedro Rodriguez, Ian Walker and many more.

Bruce left his own memorial. The outstanding Grand Prix cars of the 1980s bear the name with pride, McLaren.

As noted earlier, the one Grand Prix driver who was awarded the Segrave for success in Grand Prix racing was Jackie Stewart who was chosen for the 1973 award after winning the World Championship for drivers.

Since his retirement from the track Stewart has remained in the public eye, flying around the world from his base in Switzerland to promote business for various companies with which he is associated, mixing with royalty, judging competitions and in general being a celebrity.

His detractors say he is only interested in making money. Well, it's certainly true that Jackie has an eye for a buck or a baubee but it is also true that he is a man of honour whose word is his bond, a man who would not let down a friend and one, hobnobbing with royalty or not, who doesn't pass by the folk he met on the way up.

In that regard, surprisingly enough, he and the late Graham Hill were very similar, despite the impression Graham gave of an extrovert, wise-cracking, couldn't-care-less fellow. Graham just wasn't as business-like as Jackie.

For some years, I edited a motor-racing annual to which both Jackie and Graham were regular contributors. Never did either of them ever miss a deadline or let me down. Sometimes Jackie's copy might arrive with a note, 'Have corrected this flying over the Atlantic – will get someone to mail it to you from the airport.' Or there would be a telephone message from Graham, 'Just flying out to Mexico – can you meet me at London Airport in an hour and I'll have your copy ready for you.' Once he dictated his story to my wife who took it down in shorthand and, with years of experience taking dictation from all sorts of people, she reckoned Graham to be one of the best and most considerate.

Both men also passed the Drackett test for famous people who haven't let it go to their head – those who do not pass by and look the other way when people come along who are either not so famous of of no immediate use or both.

Several times in London streets I've been startled out of my wits by horn-blowing and turned to see a beaming Graham yelling, 'How are you, my old cock?'

And once at Silverstone my wife and I were touched when Jackie, walking along in the opposite direction with a very VIP indeed, made his apologies and trotted over to enquire after our health.

So this is the type of man who won the Segrave in 1973. The way he earned it was thus ...

He was twenty-six years of age when he won his first Grand Prix (the Italian, after a battle with team-leader Graham Hill) driving for BRM; and he was thirty when he won his first World Driver's Championship at the wheel of Ken Tyrrell's Ford-powered Matra. Still driving for Tyrrell he won the championship again in 1971 and was runner-up in 1972.

There were eleven rounds to the championship in 1973. Stewart won six of them, was second in one and fifth in another. He was in pole position six times and he set fastest lap three times.

At the end of the season, under the scoring system prevailing (five results from first six, four from second five) he had 62 points, 29 points ahead of his nearest rival, the Swedish driver Ronnie Peterson, in a March.

Peterson, in fact, did not win a race that season. The five which Jackie omitted to win went to his team-mate, François Cevert, who finished third in the championship; Jacky Ickx (Ferrari); Jo Siffert (BRM); Mario Andretti (Ferrari); and – a real surprise for British fans – Peter Gethin (BRM).

When the awarding committee reached their decision, the citation acknowledged Jackie's three championships, the fact that he had won more Grands Prix than any driver in history and also 'his constant campaign for improvements in safety standards at circuits throughout the world'.

Segrave Medals were awarded to Ken Tyrrell, team entrant; Keith Duckworth, creator of the Cosworth engine; and Mike Hewland, responsible for the Hewland gearbox. Both engine and gearbox, it was noted, were now virtually standard equipment for Formula One cars.

The six mechanics most closely associated with the car were presented with tankards.

Not long before Jackie's triumph I was asked to write his story for a Scottish newspaper, the *Sunday Mail.* This, in part, is what I said:

> Scotland's – and the world's – top racing driver, Jackie Stewart, has long hair, a highly developed sense of humour, an attractive wife, two sons and a £100,000 home in Switzerland. He also has an American manager, the famed Mark McCormack, and an income conservatively estimated at £75,000 a year.
>
> In his breakthrough years he recalls being pleased at earning £75 for one race. Today he can pick up two hundred times that amount just in winning bonuses from Goodyear whose tyres he uses.
>
> The rewards of motor-racing are great for that small elite band of Grand Prix drivers whose ranks have been thinned by death or retirement to a scant dozen or so.
>
> If Stewart repeats his 1969 Silverstone victory in this year's Woolmark British Grand Prix he will collect £2,000 first prize

money plus, possibly, up to another £1,500 for fastest laps in practice or for leading at certain stages of the race itself. But the real money comes from retainers, from entrants and engine manufacturers, tyre manufacturers and others, endorsements of products and writing books and articles and personal appearances.

Drivers and their entrants are noticeably coy about revealing their financial dealings, a trait they share with most people. Jackie Stewart, on his own statement, signed for BRM as a comparative unknown for £4,000 six years ago so his present contract with Ken Tyrrell, these six years and a World Championship later, must be worth much, much more. It certainly takes care of the bread-and-butter and, until last year, most of the jam as far as Jackie was concerned came from another contract committing him to use and test Dunlop tyres.

The Dunlop tie-up was worth £40,000 a year to Stewart but now that the Birmingham firm has pulled out of Grand Prix racing, he has a contract with the Goodyear company at an undisclosed figure.

It's all a long way from the windswept Scottish Charterhall circuit where Jackie started in club racing barely a decade ago. And even further from the Dumbuck Garage at Dumbarton, owned by Stewart Senior, where he commenced work as an apprentice mechanic at the tender age of fifteen. In those days, brother Jimmy, nine years Jackie's senior, was the racing driver in the family and a member of the Ecurie Ecosse team which brought fame, and a couple of Le Mans victories, to Scotland in the Fifties.

Jackie was more interested in clay-pigeon shooting and by 1959–60 he was good enough to collect all the home national championships. Unaccountably he missed out on Olympic selection after a poor performance in the eliminating trials.

Meanwhile brother Jimmy, after badly injuring an arm in a crash, was persuaded to give up racing.

A customer at the garage asked Jackie to drive for him in club races and the Stewart saga had begun. He raced with some success, anonymously at first since his mother was against his picking up where his brother left off, and got his big break when he was brought to the attention of a private entrant, Surrey timber merchant Ken Tyrrell.

Tyrrell phoned Jimmy Stewart and asked, 'Do you know if your brother wants to become a Grand Prix driver? Is he serious or does he do it just for fun?'

Jimmy said Jackie seemed to be serious and Tyrrell arranged

a trial at Goodwood. 'Jackie had never been in a single-seater before,' Ken recalls, 'I lectured him – I said take it steady, we've got all day.' And Jackie went out and proceeded to knock spots off the times being clocked by the great New Zealand driver, Bruce McLaren.

Signed to a contract, Stewart proceeded to mop up in Formula Three and then Formula Two until three Grand Prix teams – BRM, Lotus and Cooper – offered him terms. He opted for BRM and in his first season in the big-time won the Italian GP and gained six other places to finish third overall in the battle for the world title. He also won the non-championship International Trophy at Silverstone and, with Graham Hill as co-driver, finished tenth at Le Mans in the experimental Rover-BRM gas-turbine car. No racing driver, before or since, has made such an immediate impact.

Jackie's second big break came when in 1967 Ken Tyrrell, after years of success in the lower echelons of racing, decided the time was ripe to tackle Formula One. Jackie needed no urging to sign up with the man who had set him on the path to fame and fortune and the combination rocketed to the 1969 world title.

It was virtually over by halfway through the season. Stewart won six of the first eight Championship races that year and clinched the title in the Italian Grand Prix at Monza.

Stirling Moss and Graham Hill have always had an acute awareness of the financial possibilities inherent in their dangerous sport, a realistic appreciation of the fact that a highly skilled man, risking his life on the race circuits, is worthy of suitable reward.

But it was left to the canny Scot, Jackie Stewart, to organise himself one hundred per cent on a business basis. He made his home near Geneva, in Switzerland, a move which has obvious tax advantages. Yet he himself places more importance on the fact that being within easy reach of an international airport he can jet to anywhere in the world at a moment's notice. Air travel costs him around £20,000 a year which must put him in the more-publicised David Frost class as an airline commuter.

He picks up the telephone to call Los Angeles as casually as others dial the local butcher. He has a full-time secretary to look after his voluminous mail. And he has Mark McCormack, whose other clients include Jack Nicklaus, Arnie Palmer, Gary Player, Tony Jacklin and England cricketer Geoff Boycott.

The pressures on him are great. Demands for personal appearances, commitments for television and radio programmes, discussions with commercial sponsors and, not least, driving a very fast car better than anyone else in the world. Despite it all, Jackie remains a gentleman, a perfectionist, someone who fulfils his obligations one hundred per cent.

He would like to get out of motor-racing at the right time, suddenly and without sliding gradually down the hill into a weary sort of boring routine. When he quit shooting it was a sudden – 'and happy' – decision. He wants it the same way with motor-racing – just to wake up one morning and decide he's going to get out.

One thing for sure: 'I won't be a lost racing driver feeling that he wants to go back.'

Whatever the future holds for Jackie Stewart, flag-bearer in a chain of great Scottish competitors such as Jim Clark, Ron Flockhart and Andrew Cowan, his business acumen and shrewd investments will ensure that whenever he decides to retire, he will, unlike many of the sportsmen of the past, be able to live in comfort for the rest of his days.

Well, Jackie was again a man of his word. He retired in 1973 as World Champion and holder of the Segrave Trophy and he has resisted all attempts to lure him back. One offer was reputed to be more than £2 million.

One of his wishes did not come true. His eldest son, Paul, has become a racing-driver just as Graham Hill's son did, just as Jack Brabham's three sons did. It runs in the blood. (Jackie has apparently resigned himself to the inevitable: in July 1989 he wrote to me: 'Paul has managed to finish in the top ten in one or two races about which I am very pleased.' Since then Paul has won a race in fine style.)

A Grand Prix driver *did* win the Segrave Tropy *after* Jackie Stewart but for winning the World *Sports Car* Championship. In fact, you could say that 29-year-old Martin Brundle of King's Lynn, Norfolk, was something of a disillusioned Grand Prix driver when he was awarded the trophy in 1988.

After early successes in saloon cars and Formula Three he broke into Grand Prix racing with Stewart's old team, Tyrrell. He was fifth in his first race and second in Detroit three months later before being injured in Dallas. After a couple of seasons with Tyrrell, themselves in the doldrums, he went to

Zakspeed but became disenchanted with struggling in non-competitive machinery which had no chance of winning.

He made a bold decision in 1988 voluntarily to quit the Grand Prix circus and spend a year in sports-car racing. He signed for the works supported Tom Walkinshaw Silk Cut Jaguar team and his fifth victory of the season – at Mount Fuji – brought him the World Championship ahead of the AEG Sauber Mercedes drivers, Jean-Louis Schlesser and Mauro Baldi. It also brought Martin the Segrave Trophy ahead of double-winner Wing Commander Ken Wallis, powerboat aces Steve Curtis and Roger Fletcher and British rally champion Jimmy McRae.

For Brundle it was a gamble which paid off in more ways than one. The year 1989 saw him back in a Grand Prix single-seater. The Brabham team, after a year's sabbatical, returned to the circuits with a new owner and organization. They promptly signed Brundle as their No. 1 driver. For the veteran of fifty-five GPs it was a whole new beginning and the outlook turned distinctly rosier with a scoring place in the Monaco Grand Prix.

The only other car driver to gain the Segrave, as distinct from those motor-cyclists who also, to varying degrees, took part in car-racing and rallying, was Leicestershire rally driver, Roger Clark, Britain's outstanding rally driver of modern times.

The man who had spent so much of his life in a bucket seat concentrating on getting into the next control without being late and incurring penalty marks so nearly missed his own presentation.

With the guests assembled and everything ready, there was no sign of Roger. Getting more and more anxious by the minute I made my way down to the Entrance Hall of the RAC and asked the head porter if there had been any message. No, came the reply. I went outside into Pall Mall and saw a pedestrian dodging in and out of the fast-moving traffic. Then, as he neared the safety of the pavement, I saw with relief that it was Roger.

As we ran up the stairs – I was slimmer in those days – he breathlessly explained that traffic in most of London was impenetrable that day (it may not have been exactly the word he used) and in the end, in desperation, he had abandoned his car somewhere near Piccadilly Circus tube station and run the rest of the way to the RAC, an explanation which met with some ribald comments from his assembled colleagues.

That 1975 award was truly a team effort and a tribute to the outstanding British rally team and car of the post-war period, Ford and the Ford Escort. The citation coupled Roger's name with that of competitions director Stuart Turner, team manager Peter Ashcroft, Roger's co-driver Jim Porter who was with him many years, and the Ford Motor Company ... Rally Champions.

There should have been another name on the citation, Roger's team-mate, Timo Makinen, but Timo is Finnish and so not eligible under Segrave Trophy rules. Perhaps we should have taken the word of a certain national newspaper sub-editor who once referred to him as 'Tim McKinnon, the leading Scottish driver'. Timo, the original 'Flying Finn', had won the RAC International Rally that year of 1975 and put up a spectacular performance in the Tour de France.

Roger could only finish second in the RAC Rally in 1975 although he had been the winner in 1972 and would win again in 1976.

He was just one minute behind Timo after 72 stages which, in view of the chapter of accidents he experienced, was quite a performance. The rear hand-brake calipers seized, twice he had broken shock absorbers and twice strut failure. The hand-brake cable broke, there was a hole in the bell housing and a broken clutch fixing-bolt and the gearbox selectors came adrift, leaving him with only first and fifth gears. All these calamities happened on stages and Roger estimated they cost him seven minutes – and he lost by one.

But Ford 1-2 made Stuart Turner and Peter Ashcroft happy.

Roger *did* win the RAC Rally Championship. He won the Granite City, the Welsh, the Scottish, the Burmah, the Manx and the Lindisfarne events. He also won the South African Rally.

He retired from the Mintex Dales and the Circuit of Ireland with a blown engine and from the Antibes with suspension failure, the type of disasters to which rally drivers become accustomed.

But, in the other two rallies that he failed to finish, his troubles were somewhat unusual to say the least. At San Remo both he and Timo had to retire because they ran out of tyres. Rally cars get through an awful lot of tyres – hard-cornering, rough surfaces, stones and flints are not too good for rubber – but even so it is unusual for a team to run out. What happened in this case was that halfway across France the Dunlop truck with Ford's supply of tyres broke down and could not be repaired in time to reach San Remo for the start of the rally. Clark and Makinen started the event with just ten wheels and odd tyres between them, Makinen got a puncture almost at the start and that was that.

The Jim Clark Rally in Scotland was a different story. Roger is a slow starter – he reckons he's lazy – but a strong finisher. On this occasion he so far forgot himself as to start strongly and be the leader. On the Otterburn stages, the sheep, not yet disturbed by roaring cars, were grazing peacefully on the track when early-bird Roger appeared.

Roger couldn't stop and one of the sheep couldn't get out of the way fast enough. Roger hit it – the sort of peril Grand Prix drivers do not have to face. The car's radiator was shattered – the fate of the hapless sheep is unknown – and with twenty miles of stages to go before he could reach his service crew, Roger's rally was done.

Incidentally, Roger's car that year was sponsored by Cossack, the men's hair-spray, and Roger had to endure much leg-pulling from his mates when he appeared in the TV commercials. The Clark children apparently used Cossack on Maxwell, the family's Old English sheepdog, so perhaps Maxwell should have appeared in the commercials.

The first time I came across Roger was early in his career when he was usually driving his own cars – and winning events like the Scottish Rally. When we got back to Glasgow I was feeling tired and sore with what I was sure was a permanent disability, the result of curling my six feet into a little Hillman Imp for what seemed like years in the Scottish Highlands. When my wife and I turned up at the post-rally celebrations – a cheerful sight in themselves with pipers, kilts and a great deal of the local brew – there was another heart-warming sight: Roger and his attractive jolly wife

Judith (I think they were only engaged then) *both* happily knocking back pints of beer.

Judy (or Goo as Roger calls her) and their family have been a very stable influence in Roger's life and stability has been the key word in his rallying career. His garage-owning father greatly encouraged him, he spent almost all his career at international level with the Ford team apart from brief spells with Reliant and Rover and during that time had one man, Jim Porter, as his co-driver in the great majority of events.

The quiet and studious Porter who had been with Roger since local rally days eventually moved out of the bucket seat to be a rally organizer. Jim Porter is, in the best sense of the word, a very nice man, and Roger always valued the partnership and the friendship.

Credit for that Segrave award must also go to the management, in particular Stuart Turner, and the car, the Ford Escort.

Turner, a bespectacled graduate, first made his motor-sport name as a navigator as they were known in those far-off days when he was a young lad. And he was good enough to partner Erik Carlsson to victory in the RAC Rally. With Ford he became one of the world's great competition managers and directors.

He is also one of the world's great after-dinner speakers which might surprise those who normally see him as outwardly serious.

At a dinner at the Guildhall he brought the house down although the other speakers included TV's Frank Bough; a learned judge whom we were told was currently the best after-dinner speaker in London; and a bewildered Peter Ustinov who stood up and said, 'How do I follow that?'

Stuart makes no bones about it: 'Roger Clark is the finest rally driver Britain has ever produced.' Great drivers though Paddy Hopkirk, Pat Moss, Ian Appleyard, Peter Harper and Donald Morley were, Stuart says that none of them dominated the other British drivers as convincingly as Roger.

'He can be an awkward sod,' says Stuart, 'but we have one strong bond – we are both in love with his gorgeous wife, Judy.'

Turner was well-backed by motor sport manager Peter

Ashcroft, a Lancastrian engine expert experienced in sports and Grand Prix cars as well as rallying.

The Ford Escort is probably the world's most consistently successful car of all time. From Easter 1968, when Roger Clark's works Twin-Cam won the Circuit of Ireland, until November 1979, when Hannu Mikkola's works 2-litre RS won the RAC Rally, the cars were never out of the news and the classifications. That win of Mikkola's was in fact the eighth consecutive RAC victory for the Escort.

Then, with the withdrawal of the works team, David Sutton and Rothmans kept the legend alive, so much so that in 1981 Ari Vatanen became World Rally Champion with a model which had not officially been in production for four years.

In the late 1980s all over the world Ford Escorts were still winning rallies.

Perhaps the most remarkable sequence in a remarkable story took place between August 1975 and November 1978. During that time, starting with the Taurus rally and finishing with the Turkish Bosphorus, the Belgian driver Gilbert Staepelaere, driving an Escort RS 1800, entered 41 international rallies, won 24 of them, finished second three times and finished third five times. In the other ten he did not finish.

It is a record hardly likely to be beaten. (The American John Buffum did pass Staepelaere's record number of wins in 1987 but there is no comparison with the class of opposition the Belgian encountered.)

Truly the Ford Escort lived up to that part of the Segrave citation which refers to the possibilities of transport by land – because apart from competition successes (or perhaps because of them?) the Ford Escort became the world's best-selling car.

There was another occasion when Ford might so easily have won the award. That was in the year 1963 when the leading contenders were Eric Jackson and Ken Chambers who, in a Ford Corsair, drove around the world. They travelled a total of 43,000 miles but this included sea and air travel, their actual road distance being 30,000 miles which they covered in 24 days.

The committee were not too happy about the long distance relying on other agencies but to be fair to Eric and Ken, unless you use an amphibious craft and in some cases are accompanied by an army, it is virtually impossible to circumnavigate the globe by car.

Whatever the rights and wrongs of the affair, Eric and Ken were a little unlucky, in my view, not to receive the award.

But, as someone once said in another context, many are called, few are chosen.

6 ... *And Two*

The night of 5 September 1976. The giant Slaski Stadium in Katowiće, Poland, is jammed with 100,000 yelling Poles, Russians, Germans, a handful of Scandinavians and a sprinkling of British, Australians and New Zealanders.

The final of the World Speedway Championship is about to be decided and for the first time in many a year no Scandinavians, not even the most recent champions, Olsen (Denmark) and Michanek (Sweden) have reached the last stage.

Instead there are five Englishmen, four Poles, two Russians, an Australian, a New Zealander, a Czech, a West German and an American and the odds are on the home riders, the Poles.

Peter Collins, of Belle Vue, thinks differently. He storms through from behind to win his first heat and keeps up the pressure in his following races.

By the time of the final heat, Collins needs only second place to be sure of the title. Former World Champion New Zealander Ivan Mauger streaks away and is never headed but Collins staves off the challenge of a Russian and a Pole to become World Champion at twenty-two, the youngest rider to win the title since Peter Craven, also of Belle Vue and England, in 1955.

He also becomes only the second man on two wheels to win the coveted Segrave Trophy.

The first was a rider of 'incomparable dash and consummate stylishness', Geoffrey Duke, back in 1951. That was an eventful year for Geoff. He won the Senior and Junior Tourist Trophy Races, the Senior and Junior Belgian Grands

Prix, the Senior Dutch Tourist Trophy, the Junior French Grand Prix, the Senior and Junior German Grands Prix, the Senior and Junior Ulster Grands Prix and the Italian Junior Grand Prix, thus becoming World Champion in both 350 cc and 500 cc classes. Thus was justice done since the previous year he had lost the Senior title by just one point to Masetti, an Italian reckoned by most of the experts to be very much Geoff's inferior in sheer skill.

Duke worked at every possible angle to produce his best and even had a rubber chin-pad fitted on his tank so as to be more comfortable 'flat out'.

The gloss on his award was that his winning speed of 92.27 m.p.h. in the Senior TT shattered an eleven-year-old record but unfortunately the presentation to him the following year had to be rescheduled when he was injured during the German International Meeting at Schotten, near Frankfurt.

Someone wrote of him at the time,

> Perhaps once in a generation there appears, in the world of sport, a star so gifted that his supremacy in his particular field stands unchallenged. Such a one is Geoffrey Duke, a rider of uncanny genius, who has taken the motor-cycling world by storm. Duke is a modest, rather retiring young man of 28 from St. Helen's, Lancs, but to watch him handle his Norton in a big race is to understand how his skill and daring have led him to become a double World Champion in a mere two years of professional racing.

Earlier in the year he had ventured on to four wheels, finishing third in the Goodwood Easter Handicap, driving an Aston Martin DB3. When his injury occurred he had already amassed enough points on two wheels to retain his 350 cc World Championship, despite not being able to complete the season.

For five consecutive years Geoff was to be a World Champion although he had to switch from Norton to Gilera to do it. After retiring from riding he at one time ran his own team with bikes loaned by Gilera and Derek Minter and John Hartle as riders. In 1963 he was one of the drivers when a Mk II Jaguar of 3.8 litres set four International Class C Records at Monza, Italy, covering 10,000 miles at an average speed of 106 m.p.h.

Geoff settled in the Isle of Man, appropriately enough, and acquired a ferry service. In view of the distance he has to travel, his frequent appearances at Segrave presentations are doubly welcome.

As we said earlier, Geoff's own presentation was delayed owing to the injuries he received in Germany. In fact, it was not until December of the following year that the presentation took place, the trophy being handed over to Geoff by a famous name from between the wars, the former race-driver Sir Algernon Lee Guinness, who was at that time chairman of the Segrave Awarding Committee.

In the years that followed, motor-cyclists such as Phil Read were often considered for the trophy but not until Collins's speedway triumph did one of them actually get it. Ironically, the closest rival to Collins that year was a road-racing motor-cyclist, Barry Sheene who, despite crashing at Snetterton just before the vital sixth Grand Prix in Sweden, won the World 500 cc Championship.

Sheene's turn would not be long delayed. The following year he again won the World Championship and this time the Segrave Trophy went with it. In 1984 he would win it again when he triumphed over terrible injuries to return to international motor-cycling against all the prognostications of the medical profession. In between Sheene's two awards another great road-racer, Mike Hailwood, received the Segrave in 1979.

What tipped the balance in Collins's favour in 1976 was that he was astride a British machine. Peter's bike was powered by a Weslake engine which now took over from the Czech Jawa which had dominated speedway in the post-war years.

There was a nice twist in the tail to the Peter Collins's story. Peter had put forward the name of his entrant and engine-tuner Dave Nourish for consideration as a recipient of the Segrave Medal and the committee had no hesitation in agreeing. Of all motorized sports speedway probably makes more demands on its engine experts than most.

At the presentation the turn-out was impressive. Scores of

top riders came along to honour the jockey-sized (5 ft 7 in, 10 stone) World Champion including the runner-up, Malcolm Simmons. Then there was Angela, Peter's wife of just a few months, his mother Eileen and the family. Peter had a sister Ann and four brothers – Leslie, Philip, Neil and Stephen – all of whom became speedway riders. The brothers, that is – Ann settled for show-jumping although she did once take part in a novelty speedway race.

Despite the happy atmosphere, Peter and Dave seemed faintly troubled. Then it came out. They felt Harry Weslake, octogenarian designer and builder of the Weslake speedway engine, ought to be among the celebrants.

'Why didn't you put his name forward for a medal?' we asked. It transpired that they had been under the impression that only one Segrave Medal could be awarded whereas of course up to six medals can be given, at the committee's discretion.

Cutting a long story short, for the first and only time thus far, the committee met again to consider, not the award of the trophy, but the award of a medal. It was agreed unanimously that Harry Weslake was entitled to the medal if any man was and some months later a special presentation was arranged and Lord Camden handed over a medal to the delighted Harry.

Another good friend, Jeff Clew, wrote Harry's biography, *Lucky All My Life*, a title which embodied the optimistic and cheerful nature of a man who had a good share of downs as well as ups in his long life. Alas, the grand old man died before the book was completed but his widow, Mary, helped Jeff to complete the task and my copy of the book is inscribed by Mary, her son, Michael Daniel, who carried on the Weslake business, and his wife, Colleen, and Dave and Jean Nourish, all of them regular attenders at the Segrave presentations.

Jeff's book was a revelation to me and, I suspect, many other people who had never realized what a significant role Harry had played in many of the major developments in transport and motor sport.

From 1918 when, with his father, he filed a patent for an improved carburettor, until 1974, when he patented a spark-ignition combustion system, a constant flow of inventions and applications came from Harry's fertile brain, nearly all of them concerned with improving the performance of the internal combustion engine.

George Brough, of Brough Superior fame, used Harry's carburettors in breaking a series of world motor cycle records at Brooklands in 1922 as did other two-wheel record-breakers in Belgium, Italy and elsewhere. From then on Harry practically lived at the Weybridge track and did so well as an entrant in motor-cycle events that Sunbeams entered into an agreement with him. In 1926 came a setback. Harry had supplied a lot of equipment to a certain manufacturer who went bankrupt – before paying Harry's bill. Lack of cash-flow forced him to close down his own company but it turned out a blessing in disguise. As an automotive consultant he was soon in demand. W. O. Bentley called for his services. So did Leonard Lord, of Austin and Wolseley; William Lyons, of SS, soon to be Jaguar; Citroën; Armstrong-Siddeley; Alta racing cars. The list was almost endless.

He was even approached by a smooth-talking man who turned out to be the leader of a gang of crooks and who figured that Harry was just the man to tune the getaway car.

During the Second World War Harry worked on Rolls-Royce aircraft engines, US Mustangs and even the Cromwell tank and afterwards he set up his own company at premises in Rye, Sussex, which were to become a permanent home for Weslake Engineering.

It would – and has – taken a book (*Lucky All My Life*) to describe all of Harry's subsequent achievements. To name but a few – Norton motor-cycles, Jaguar XK120 sports cars, the record-breaking Goldie Gardner Special, Austin-Healey, Connaught-Alta racing cars, Daimlers, the successful Grand Prix car team of Tony Vandervell – all of these contained modifications and improvements designed by Weslake.

Then came the Gurney-Weslake Grand Prix engine used by Dan Gurney's All-American Racers, the Eagles, who set up shop at the Rye factory. Work on Ford cars followed and led to the European Touring Car Championship in 1971. So you see Harry Weslake might easily have won a dozen Segrave

Medals in his long career. But he preferred to stay in the background gaining his pleasure from his work.

The Weslake speedway engine not only revolutionized the sport but played a major role in helping British riders to the top. When Peter Collins won the world title on Weslake, runner-up Malcolm Simmons was also Weslake-mounted. John Louis won the 1977 British Championship on Weslake and Colin Richards won the National League Championship. Eastbourne Eagles, Champions of the National League, proudly proclaimed, 'Raced on Weslake Engines'.

I last saw Harry to speak to at Silverstone in the summer of 1978. He was in good form. 'Come and have a drink,' he said and promptly led the way into the nearest hospitality tent where he was greeted like a long lost brother. We talked about the future – Harry was a man who preferred to look ahead rather than back – and made tentative arrangements for a visit to Rye. (Michael Daniel has often repeated the invitation and to my regret I still haven't been.)

I next saw him – in the distance – at the Golden Jubilee World Speedway Championship at Wembley on the night of Saturday, 2 September 1978. Harry had several Weslake runners – Malcolm Simmons, Gordon Kennett, Dave Jessup and the American, Scott Autrey – and when I spotted him he was right by the safety-fence near the pits scrutinizing them all very carefully.

In the sequel the Jawa-mounted Dane, Ole Olsen, won the title for the third time but Kennett was second and Autrey third. Moreover, Autrey, Lee and finally Jessup all set new track records.

Those were the final achievements of a great man. With the end of the meeting Harry and Mary started to wend their way to the après-championships shindig. Harry staggered and fell. He was dead by the time the ambulance reached hospital.

I doubt whether we shall see his like again. Geniuses are usually said to be mad or irascible or both, but Harry Weslake was lovable.

Great night of triumph and nostalgia though it was, that Golden Jubilee meeting was doubly tinged with sadness because, only a few hours before it began, Charles Foot, President of the British League, died in his hotel room. He was a shrewd man who had played a great part in the revival of British speedway.

Speedway paid its own tribute to Harry Weslake. The Dugard family, who operated the Eastbourne track, staged the Weslake Memorial Meeting which was better than any eulogy or memorial stone. Harry would have liked that ...

Peter Collins retired young from the sport but he compressed some remarkable achievements into a comparatively short space of time. He captained England and, apart from winning the World Championship in 1976, he was runner-up in 1977 and World Masters Champion in 1978. He was European Champion in 1974, Inter-Continental Champion 1976 and 1977 and British Champion 1979. He was also a member of the winning combination in the World Pairs Championship in 1977 and 1980 and the World Team Championship in 1973, 1974, 1975, 1977 and 1980, a formidable record.

When he received the Segrave Peter told me he had three dislikes – traffic jams, getting up in the morning and *being beaten*.

It is the spirit which all Segrave Trophy recipients have and the reason why, when Peter was nominated by the Sports Writers Association as one of their Sportsmen of the Year but could not attend, I was happy and proud to receive the award on his behalf.

The Barry Sheene Segrave presentations were also family affairs and very happy occasions. The first award was straightforward enough – Sheene had narrowly missed the award the previous year and when he won the World Championship for the second year in succession his claim was irrefutable. The second – in 1984 – was rather different and the committee discussed the matter for a very long time before coming to a decision. Sheene's career as a motor-cyclist was over and he had just announced his retirement.

He was *not* nominated to mark his retirement but his courage. In 1982 he shattered both legs in a horrific crash at Silverstone and only masterly surgery during a seven-hour operation saved them, yet Sheene amazed medical opinion by his sheer courage, self-discipline and determination to ride again.

Despite having four metal plates and twenty-three screws holding his limbs together, Sheene was riding a 500 cc world championship machine the following season.

The award was duly agreed and met with acclaim in the motor-cycling world and beyond it. It was obvious when this second presentation was made that Barry had pulled through not only because of his own determination but because of the support he received from the lovely Stephanie and his Mum and Dad, amateur road-racers Frank and Iris. (When Barry was born, the overjoyed Frank had told all and sundry, 'I've just been presented with the winner of the 1970 TT.')

And, as Peter Pitchford, of Castrol, said in handing over the trophy, Barry's 'sense of humour in difficult situations' must have helped. Some difficult situation. Some sense of humour.

A comeback also earned Mike Hailwood the Segrave Trophy in 1979. For determination, 'Mike the Bike' was not a whit behind Barry Sheene.

Fourteen times a Tourist Trophy winner, Mike had retired from motor-cycle racing to pursue a Grand Prix career in cars. (Coincidentally, Geoff Duke and Barry Sheene also took up car racing with varying degrees of success.) Mike became an established competitor, a regular on the circuit, without ever achieving the dominance he had enjoyed in two-wheel sport.

When he did hit the headlines it was not for winning a race.

It happened during the 1973 South African Grand Prix. The Swiss driver, Clay Regazzoni, crashed in a 'flamer'. Hailwood stopped and despite the grave risk to himself, dragged Regazzoni from the burning car, undoubtedly saving his life.

He was awarded the George Medal, one of Britain's highest honours for civilian bravery.

Then, after he himself had a terrible crash in the 1974 German Grand Prix, Mike retired from motor-racing. One of his legs was 'bent like a banana' and his right foot was locked flat and had little movement, something which effectively prevented him from driving a Grand Prix car to the maximum. Nine-times World Motor-cycling Champion he admitted to never quite mastering the cars and his only four-wheeled championship was the European Formula Two title, which would have been a great honour for lesser men.

Yet something calls the Hailwoods of this world. In June

1978, eleven years after he quit the bikes, Mike returned to the Isle of Man. He could still ride a motor-cycle providing the gear-change was switched to the left-hand side of the machine – and he proved it. On a privately entered Ducati he won the Formula One race, beating Mick Grant and the works Hondas of Phil Read and John Williams, and breaking the lap and circuit records. Sadly, his father, Stan, who had played an important role in Mikes's career, had died a couple of months earlier.

He wasn't satisfied – and went back in 1979. He was fifth in the Formula One race, despite losing top gear and his battery; first in the Senior Tourist Trophy; and beaten by a matter of seconds in the Classic, probably the finest and closest fought race the island has ever seen.

The Classic promised a nose-to-nose struggle – and lived up to the promise. With £30,000 prize-money at stake, this 226-mile race brought together the winner of the Formula One race – Alex George; and the victor in the Senior TT – Mike Hailwood.

In the early laps George had a lead which varied between just three or four seconds but when Hailwood launched his challenge he nosed ahead of his rival by just one second. George fought back and when Hailwood ran into delays negotiating back markers George won by just 3.4 seconds.

Hailwood's comeback had underlined that he was probably the greatest motor-cycle racer of them all.

In announcing their award, the Segrave Committee praised his 'immaculate attitude – which has set a fine example to all youngsters taking up the sport'.

There was one very unique aspect of Hailwood's year. One often hears of sportsmen and journalists being at loggerheads but in this case Mike Hailwood made a special request that a Segrave Medal be awarded to a sports-writer.

Northern motor-cycling journalist Ted Macauley, already honoured by the Auto-Cycle Union as 'the motor-cycling journalist of the year' was the man who persuaded Mike to come out of retirement and return to the scenes of his great triumphs in the Isle of Man. Macauley obtained bikes and sponsorship and masterminded the comeback. 'We were a team,' said Macauley. 'I made the pass, Mike scored the winner.'

Mike Hailwood was more definite, 'Without Ted it would not have been possible.'

Sadly, Mike, who had survived all sorts of crashes on two wheels and four, died in a road accident which was not his fault.

I treasure a copy of the story of his comeback, *Mike the Bike – Again*, inscribed by Mike and Ted.

Jackie Stewart (*second from the left*) judging a Goodyear Tyre Competition in 1977. Fellow judges included the author (*extreme left*) and motoring-correspondent Pat Mennem (*third from right*)

Jackie Stewart cornering in the Monaco Grand Prix

Roger Clark in a Ford Escort on his way to winning the 1972 RAC Rally, the first British driver to do so since Gerry Burgess in 1959 who also drove a Ford

'Unaccustomed as I am to public speaking . . .' Barry Sheene expresses his thanks after receiving the Segrave Trophy

Peter Collins, world speedway champion (*centre*) flanked by explorer John Blashford-Snell, speedboat record-breaker Lady Arran, his own engine-tuner and entrant Dave Nourish, autogyro world record-breaker Ken Wallis and test pilot John Cunningham

The man who 'breathed on engines', Harry Weslake, receives a special Segrave Medal from the Marquess Camden

Lady Arran and co-pilot Roger Trigg in joyful mood after their successful record attempt during which they exceeded 100 m.p.h.

Richard Branson and his crew (Atlantic oarsman Chay Blyth is third from left) after being awarded the Segrave Trophy for the fastest ever crossing of the Atlantic

Wing-Commander Ken Wallis in one of his tiny autogyros

Explorer John Blashford-Snell with Segrave plaque and trophy

Rear-Admiral Sandy Woodward shows colleagues the Segrave plaque awarded to him and members of the British Falklands Task Force

Lady Camden with 'Brecky', breaker of waterspeed records and a great friend of Segrave's

Stuart Bladon with the Citroën AX Diesel, new world fuel economy record holder for production vehicles

The Marquess Camden with Lord Mountbatten and HRH Prince Charles at Brands Hatch

7 *Across the Waters*

The two Campbells, Cobb, Eyston, Peter Twiss and Roger Clark have all taken to the water as well as their more usual pursuits but it was not until 1980 that a powerboat racer, pure and simple, won the Segrave Trophy. And when it did happen the recipient was only the third woman to win the trophy.

Lakes and ponds seem to have played an important role in the life of Fiona, Lady Arran: when she gets excited she jumps into them. It began years ago when she was the 'pin-up' girl of the boys of Eton and climaxed a dance by stripping to her underwear and diving into the local pond.

Forty years on she was still doing it. When she brought her neat blue-and-white powerboat *Trimite Skean Dhu* alongside the jetty and was told that she had taken the World Class II Record and had become the first woman to exceed 100 m.p.h. on water, there seemed only one thing to do. Fiona did it. She jumped fully clothed into the dark and murky waters of Lake Windermere.

Her co-pilot, a mere male named Roger Trigg, could hardly do less – and into the water he went.

Hauled out of the water, the noble lady celebrated in more conventional fashion with some champagne.

She had reason to celebrate. Not only had she beaten the American ace, Betty Cooke, to the magic 100 but she had done it at an age when most women's idea of excitement is the Women's Institute. Fiona would never see sixty again and she was also a grandmother.

The remarkable story of a remarkable woman began in Scotland. She was the daughter of a Scottish knight, Sir Iain

Colquhoun, once known as 'the uncrowned king of Scotland', but a land impoverished soldier for all that.

Sir Iain had thousands of acres but very little money.

> We used to live off the land – rabbits, deer and fish, [says Lady Arran] but if we wanted things we had to make do. Once we decided we wanted a boat and we were simply told to go and make one, which we did by tying some old logs together.
>
> But I was always potty about speed. When I was about seven I had a bicycle and used to cycle each day along Loch Lomondside to the village. I carried a stopwatch in my hand and timed myself. Each day I tried to knock seconds off my previous fastest time.
>
> By the time I was ten I was allowed to drive cars on the estate where I couldn't do much harm but I was dying to get out on the open road and let things rip.
>
> I tried to drive as fast as I could and imagined I was a crack test pilot or racing-driver. In fact, I much preferred aeroplanes to dolls as presents.
>
> Eventually I managed to get out on the road without anyone spotting me and off I shot to the village. To my horror the village policeman was standing on a corner but as I went by he shut his eyes and nothing was ever said to my father.

At eighteen, Fiona met and married her husband. 'Boofy', as he was known to his intimates, holder of an Irish peerage, was a character in his own right.

Perhaps surprisingly for two such strong personalities the marriage endured. They were together for approaching fifty years in 'a good loving fighting marriage … the only kind to have. And a very successful marriage, thank heavens'.

'Boofy' was the more temperamental of the two and Fiona tended to let him take command although sometimes there were fierce arguments.

> He had this hot Irish temper and yet he was terribly generous. But he used to create frightful scenes which we learned to anticipate from the look on his face. The whole family would march out of a restaurant and wait outside while he had one and come back when it was over and finish our meal. We were frightful cowards.
>
> One generous gift was when, knowing my love of speed, he

> very kindly bought me an E-type Jaguar which was supposed to go at 150 m.p.h. I tried it on the motorway but to my annoyance it would only go at 149 m.p.h. We sent it back and they got it to do that extra mile. After that I seemed to be doing 150 m.p.h. quite often.

Were the police still shutting their eyes?

'The less said the better about that although I did once get away with doing ninety down Oxford Street with six people in a two-seater after a party. But that was in the small hours of the morning and there was no one about.'

The Arrans' home life came under the public eye. For years Lord Arran wrote a highly entertaining column in the London *Evening News* in which his chief targets were Swiss bankers, 'the little gnomes of Zurich', as he called them.

From time to time he would refer to life at home at 'Pimlico', his Hertfordshire home built in the 1920s. Thus *Evening News* readers became familiar with Lady Arran's activities and with those of the badgers which had the run of the place. They still do. And from time to time they appropriate the Sunday joint from the refrigerator. Llamas and wallabies are also to be seen at Pimlico, very useful for keeping the grass down.

With the children grown up and Lord Arran's job keeping him out to all hours, Fiona badly felt the need for something to do.

'I was very old, nearly fifty, when I first heard about power-boating. It really tickled my fancy and I became a fiend for it.'

She soon made the grade. With her boats *Badger I* and *Badger II* she was in the British team for the 1966 Paris Six Hours Race and for the 1967 Rouen 24 Hours Race in which she finished sixth.

With a foot down, flat-out style, she soon took the world record for standard production powerboats but her bid to be first to the 100 m.p.h. mark seemed doomed to failure. Ten times she passed 90 m.p.h. but failed to reach the ton – 'The water was thick and lifeless, it badly needed rain.'

She remained her cheerful ebullient self. 'I practised in my car on the motorway and I realized that 100 m.p.h. wasn't really very fast at all.'

Eventually in August 1980 she made it, but only after a new engine was installed the night before the attempt, her crew having to make a thousand-miles round trip to get it.

Thus she earned the Segrave Trophy with co-pilot Trigg and chief mechanic John Leighton being awarded Segrave Medals.

A few days before she was due to receive the trophy, Lady Arran telephoned me and mentioned that she had fallen from her horse. Alarmed that the star turn might not be present I enquired if she was badly injured. 'No, I was lucky,' she chuckled, 'I fell on my head.'

At the presentation, journalists asked her to describe her record attempt. She said,

> The lake was a bit choppy and it had rained before so the water was aerated and really good. It was actually raining during the attempt which was really painful at that speed. We made the first run and we knew we had done 106 m.p.h. The patrol boat was filled with people waving their arms and cheering. We had to take a five-minute break before the return trip and the agony from the rain hitting my eyes was terrible. Both goggles were blown off from the speed. I didn't think that there would be much difference in speed between 95 and 106 but there is – it really is much faster. Our second run was not so good – only about 98 so that brought the average down to 102. The old steam boat blew her horn and the other boats joined in. People were cheering and a convoy escorted us back to shore. The champagne flowed – *and our team of three people had swelled to about one hundred.*

There is a slight air of wistfulness, of regret that she hasn't gone even faster when Lady Arran reflects, 'I suppose the trouble is that I started when I was too old,' to which the editor of *Powerboat Magazine* retorted: 'Lady Arran may think she is too old but her record stands as an example that life begins at 60 and illustrates that sheer determination makes all impossibilities possible.'

And so say all of us.

At this point in time there has been one other powerboat winner of the Segrave Trophy and his exploits were summed up by Castrol's Derek Hancocks when he presented the trophy. He said:

> Today we honour a remarkable man, Richard Branson, entrepreneur, business tycoon, Mr Clean of London, record-breaker extraordinary and the subject of today's award.
>
> All this achieved in just thirty years or so. The similarities in determination, motivation, skill and courage of Sir Henry Segrave and Richard Branson make it overwhelmingly proper that he should today be awarded the trophy.
>
> He joins an illustrious group of people who have, over the years, earned the admiring respect of the nation by their exploits. I am sure I will be forgiven for not reciting the full list but for those joining us for the first time, can I give you just a taste of past winners: Amy Johnson and Jean Batten, the intrepid lady fliers; the family firm of Malcolm and Donald Campbell; and John Cobb, all familiar names of yesteryear.
>
> And from the recent past Ken Wallis, Stirling Moss, Lady Arran and John Cunningham, all of whom are with us today.
>
> All these notable people have added to the prestige of the Segrave Trophy. And now a new dynamic force will lend his worldwide appeal to carry the award to a new and younger generation.
>
> Richard demonstrated his entrepreneurial flair early on. At the age of eighteen he was proprietor and editor of *Student* magazine when most of that age invest their energies almost exclusively in the pursuit of pleasure. A frank remark reported at that time was that his 'main aim is survival'.
>
> In a business sense that is amusing, looking from today's perspective. However, in the realms of record-breaking, survival must register quite high in the minds of those taking part. At this point we should pay tribute to the survivors – the crew, who bravely shared the risks, the fears (I presume they did have some) and the success – Chay Blyth, Dag Pike, Peter McCann, Steve Ridgway, Ecki Rastig and Steve Lawes.
>
> To make the second attempt more poignant, bear in mind the first attempt was dashed a few hundred miles from home when the boat sank after striking flotsam. Undeterred, can you believe it, they volunteered a second time and with great success.
>
> At this point I am reminded of a quote, one of Richard's quotes – 'My business philosophy seeks to do the world some

good by persuading other companies to treat their employees more sympathetically.' Well, I imagine the team needed all the sympathy it could get in mid-Atlantic, bashing and crashing about at over 60 m.p.h.

And in this fashion the Segrave Trophy was handed to Richard Branson and medals to his crew in recognition of their feat in crossing the Atlantic in three days, 8 hrs and 40 mins in the powerboat *Virgin Atlantic Challenger II*, roughly 1,000 miles a day.

The United States Merchant Marine Academy, guardians of the Hales Blue Riband Trophy for the fastest Atlantic crossing refused to relinquish the trophy, previously won in 1952 by the revolutionary turbine liner, the *United States*. Branson's powerboat was dismissed as 'a toy'.

I wonder if the lady who said that genuinely believes that it is tougher to cross the Atlantic in a luxury liner weighing 53,300 tons than in a speedboat of four tons. But then the Americans don't relinquish trophies lightly as Australian and New Zealand yachtsmen have found out.

Branson didn't stop to argue – he was too busy crossing the Atlantic – in a balloon.

Postscript

Three years after Richard Branson's fastest Atlantic crossing, American millionaire Tom Gentry, with a crew of five, in a British-built boat, beat Richard's time by almost 18½ hours. Richard was on hand at St Mary's Quay to present the American with the Virgin Atlantic Challenge Trophy. Said Richard: 'I admire you enormously.' Said Gentry: 'You are a sport.'

Part III
Following the Flag

More often than not, the Segrave Trophy has been awarded to men and women in the mould of Segrave himself – air pioneers, Grand Prix drivers, record-breakers on land and water. Yet every now and again someone comes along who does not fit tidily into one or more of these categories. Theirs are the stories which follow.

8 *Where the Trails Run Out*

The natives were reported hostile so the leader of the expedition distributed arms to his force and ordered a sharp look-out, especially where the jungle came down to the edge of the river.

When danger did come, it came not from the jungle but from the river itself. Without warning, one of the leading boats plunged into an abyss, going down into a great hole on the far side of an enormous boulder, over which water poured in a torrent. Unable to stop, the craft carrying the leader followed.

The engine cut out as the water hit it, ropes were loosened and equipment washed overboard. Then, miraculously, the craft was flung clear of the hole and into less turbulent waters. The next boat in line managed to skirt the danger but the last one also plunged into the abyss, standing on end for a horrifying moment before crashing back right side up.

Another expedition had made but four miles in the day owing to heavy rain, thunder and lightning. When the storm ceased they set off again in their heavily loaded canoes but the storm returned and two canoes were lost and two men drowned, four guns going with them into the depths of the river.

Those two expeditions were a hundred years apart but the river which was 'the villain of the piece' was the same river in both cases.

The second of them – but the first in time – was led by the journalist H. M. Stanley, the man who searched for and found the missing missionary-explorer Dr Livingstone, their meeting and Stanley's 'Dr Livingstone, I presume?' being one of the best-remembered meetings in history. Stanley was the first man to explore the River Congo.

The other expedition was led by a regular soldier, Major (later Colonel) John Blashford-Snell, and it 'followed in Stanley's footsteps' along the river which modern African politicians had renamed the Zaire.

The man who led it has become one of the most famous of latterday explorers. Known irreverently as 'Blashers' to his intimates.

Tall, dark, wavy-haired and varying from trim moustache to full beard and clean-shaven, 'Blashers' is a boys' fiction hero come to life. Hailing from a seafaring family, with Oliver Cromwell and 'Hanging Judge' Jeffreys lurking around the family tree for good measure, he was driven by the urge to explore from boyhood.

He became a professional soldier, saw active service in Cyprus and Ulster, but found his true niche as an instructor at the Sandhurst Military Academy with special responsibility for Adventure Training. In this capacity, he organized more than sixty expeditions to all parts of the world and himself took part in a dozen or more.

Underwater exploration in the Mediterranean and treks across the North African desert were followed by ventures into Ethiopia including the Great Abbai Expedition which made the first descent and scientific exploration of the Blue Nile. A further expedition was to the little-known Dahlak Islands of the Red Sea.

A still greater challenge came in 1971–2 when he led the British Trans-American Expedition across the Darien Gap in Panama and Colombia, terrain which can only be described as fearsome. 'Blashers' lost a half-pint of blood on this expedition when he was attacked by a vampire bat.

Hardly had the Darien Gap mission been set up than the Zaire River Expedition was proposed by Richard Snailham, who had been a member of the Great Abbai Expedition and written a book on it, *The Blue Nile Revealed*.

It took four years to launch the new venture. The Scientific Exploration Society, of which Blashford-Snell is chairman, backed the idea from the start and a year later Prince William of Gloucester announced it to the world at a dinner in the

City. (Prince William hoped to go on the expedition himself but, alas, that was not to be.) Announcing it was one thing, turning the dream into reality quite another.

The objectives were clear and understandable. Stanley had set out from Zanzibar in November 1874 and reached the Atlantic coast of Africa in August 1877, but no detailed scientific work was carried out and nearly a hundred years later the vast Congo Basin remained largely inaccessible. The new expedition would hope to remedy some of those matters and was timed to set forth in 1974 so as to commemorate the centenary of Stanley's journey.

The problems were something else again. To start with there were the logistics of taking some 120 people, including a large body of scientists, down 2,718 miles of river, much of it dangerous rapids-strewn tracts not normally traversed. There was an even bigger headache. The question of Zaire's government which, in Snailham's words, had 'de-baptized' Stanley, torn down his statue and renamed all streets and towns associated with the great explorer.

Such difficulties were all in a day's work to Blashford-Snell and his colleagues.

More than £100,000 had to be raised in cash and equipment; a team of 165 assembled, most of them Britons but including Americans, Canadians, New Zealanders, Belgians, French, Nepalese, Fijians, a contingent from Zaire itself, and a solitary Dane. Among such a mixed party there were naturally some strange encounters. 'Blasher's' PA, Pamela Baker, met Fijian Corporal Signaller, Sam Qarau, who said, 'Baker? That's interesting, my grandfather ate a missionary named Baker.'

D-Day was set for 4 October 1974.

Snailham's vivid pen described the arrival in Zaire thus:

> It was a scenario that Cubby Broccoli [producer of the James Bond films] would have been proud of. With its lights probing the runway a DC10 of Air Zaire had come down to make a night landing at Lubumbashi airport. It could have been James Bond that appeared at the head of the floodlit disembarkation platform but instead it was the pro-consular Victorian figure of Lieutenant-Colonel John Blashford-Snell,

the uniformed topeed leader of the Zaire River Expedition, 1974–75.

What else to expect from a man whom Graham Lord in the *Sunday Express* described as 'one of the last great British explorers, adventurers and eccentrics'.

The end of the journey when the expedition had navigated the length of the river and reached its goal, the Atlantic Ocean, was described by 'the pro-consul' himself:

> Two days later at dusk, the strange fleet that had set out almost four months before in the centre of Africa, sailed into the setting sun. Our padre, in cassock and surplice, held an improvised cross and beneath the flags of nations represented on the expedition he conducted a simple service. Under our hulls, the water heaved gently, strangely it no longer pulled and tugged at us, there was no current, we were in the Atlantic.

What would Stanley have thought? He had said, 'There is no feat that any other explorer will attempt what we have done in the cataract region. It would be insanity.'

Insanity or not, Blashford-Snell and his team had attempted it and had succeeded. As their leader commented, 'We had come not to conquer Zaire, or its people, but to fight the invisible enemy of disease and to discover the scientific secrets of this vast land.'

The Segrave Trophy Committee described it as, 'the first major scientific navigation of the Zaire', and awarded Segrave Medals to Captain M. G. Gambier, late Royal Marines (Deputy Leader); Major D. T. Jackson, Intelligence Corps (Support Group Commander); Major G. R. Mitchell, BEM, Scots Guards (Quarter-Master); Captain P. J. Marett, Royal Engineers (Intelligence Officer); Captain J. Masters, Royal Engineers (Chief Engineer – Boats); and Warrant-Officer 1 C. T. Taylor, Army Air Corps (AAC Detail Commander and Chief Pilot).

Warrant-Officer Taylor was a veteran of Blashford-Snell expeditions and presumably occasionally found time to pursue his hobbies – collecting butterflies.

In addition to the Segrave awards, Corporal Neil Rickard

was awarded the Queen's Gallantry Medal for saving the crew of an Avon recce boat sucked under by a whirlpool.

For John Blashford-Snell the work of exploration and of training the young and broadening their horizons goes on. At the time of the Zaire River Expedition he was comparatively unknown outside Service and exploration circles. Since then his work on Operation Drake and Operation Raleigh has made him famous worldwide.

His brushes with death continue. During Operation Drake, John and some of his colleagues were off Papua-New Guinea in the brigantine *Eye of the Wind*, when they spotted a school of sperm whales.

He ordered the ship's inflatable dinghy to be launched so they could film the whales as they leapt clear of the water only four hundred yards away. They cut the outboard engine and paddled close to the school. There were six of them in the inflatable, including John, Major Frank Esson and Robyn Horley, a young lady who was operating the film camera.

The whales appeared to take no notice. The school seemed to be mainly cows although there were a few young ones.

But the bull was cruising slightly below the main herd. Suddenly it surfaced and its tail whipped into the air.

The local fishermen call the sperm whale's tail 'the hand of death' because so many small boats have been crushed by it.

> We quickly realized the situation was very serious [said 'Blashers']. The bull, which we estimate was nearly 50 feet long, was coming at us like a train, thrashing its tail. Major Esson tried to start the outboard motor but it wouldn't go. By now I was really worried. I began to feel like Captain Ahab in Moby Dick. In the nick of time the motor fired and we leapt away with the whale's head right under us and his back cutting a great bow wave in the water. It was a truly terrifying experience. I have had close calls with charging elephants, rhinos and crocodiles but this was the most frightening attack I have ever seen. If we had waited any longer we would have been lifted out of the water on his back and probably smashed to death by his tail.

John Blashford-Snell once again lived to tell the tale and once again was soon planning another expedition. For men like him there is always some corner of the Earth needing exploration which means that although he sometimes attends the annual Segrave reunion and presentation, more often a telegram like this one received in 1978 arrives instead of him: 'MY HUSBAND IS IN PANAMA BUT I KNOW WOULD SEND GOOD WISHES. JUDITH BLASHFORD-SNELL.'

That one meant that he was well advanced with Operation Drake – leading groups of young explorers around the world in emulation of the circumnavigation of the globe by Sir Francis Drake four hundred years previously.

9 *Will the Real James Bond Please Stand Up?*

If John Blashford-Snell is the trophy winner reminiscent of a Victorian James Bond, then Wing-Commander Ken Wallis, pilot extraordinary, is the modern Bond – but a Bond with a difference. Ken does not have to rely on a civil servant for his complex machinery, devices, guns and aircraft – he invents them himself. In fact, in addition to a flavour of Bond, Ken also has a touch of the mad inventor beloved in comic books, as anyone who has visited his rambling mansion in Norfolk will testify. Come to think of it, his wife Peggy and his family would also testify to it. They love horses and are a bit puzzled by the old boy's preoccupation with things mechanical.

Ken's study is a mass of books, papers, odd inventions (like his miniature 1½-in revolver which actually fires real bullets), blueprints etc. If you want to sit down, you may well have to shift an aircraft propeller – or even an engine.

Outside there has been a fair division. A line of stables for the female members of the family; an aircraft hanger for Ken.

He was awarded the Segrave Trophy in 1968 for his 'courage, initiative and skill in the course of developing the ultra light autogyro and demonstrating its possibilities'.

Behind that simple statement lies an extraordinary story.

Ken Wallis was born at Ely (Cambs) in 1916 into a family who were already entranced with the idea of flight, his father and uncle having constructed an all-metal monoplane in 1910. Ken had a pilot's licence by the time he was twenty-one and served throughout the Second World War as an operational pilot flying Lysanders and – on 36 bombing operations – Wellingtons.

Specializing in air armament, he stayed in the RAF on a permanent commission after the war and a number of his ideas and inventions in the armament field were adopted by the Services. His abiding interest, however, was the design of the ultra-light autogyro and in 1963 the first Wallis craft of this type made its maiden flight.

What is an autogyro? It is a rotary-winged aircraft in which the rotor-blades rotate aerodynamically, in the manner of a sycamore seed. It has the advantage of safety, simplicity and liveliness but it cannot truly hover in the manner of a helicopter with which it is often confused. Virtually all major autogyro development has taken place in Great Britain, the first practical craft of its type being built before the war by the Cierva Autogiro Company which bore the name of the machine's inventor, a Spaniard named Juan de la Cierva, who first flew his autogyro on 9 January 1923 and died in an air crash at Croydon.

Sizes have varied from the tiny Weir machine, another pre-war effort, to the mighty Fairey Rotodyne, which operated as an autogyro in its 200 m.p.h. forward flight.

In 1963, Ken Wallis's first machine could take off in 75 ft and then climb to 1,000 ft in less than a minute. With normal tanks it could carry enough fuel for two or three hours' flying.

With the success of this aircraft, Ken retired from the RAF to devote his full time to the project. The years since have been packed with more action than most men see in a lifetime.

That maiden flight earned him the Alan Marsh Medal from the Royal Aeronautical Society and five years later came the Segrave. Meanwhile, record after record fell before those spinning sycamore seeds:

- the World Altitude Record at 4,678.58 metres, nearly twice the height of the existing American-held record;
- the World Speed Record, again previously held by the Americans and bettered by Wallis by nearly 30 m.p.h.; he notched up 168 k.p.h. (104 m.p.h.) against the 127 k.p.h. (79 m.p.h.) of a Benson B-8M, powered by a 90 hp engine whereas the Wallis engine was only 60 hp.

Ken Wallis continued to break records in the ensuing years and in 1985 he was awarded the trophy for the second time 'for his achievement in gaining *all* the world autogyro records in an aircraft of his own design and construction'.

In making the presentation on the latter occasion, Peter Pitchford, managing director of Burmah-Castrol (UK) Ltd, pointed out that in 1929 an Imperial Airways Argosy flew from Paris to London in 1 hr and 45 mins which was a record at the time for the 8-ton aircraft carrying 20 passengers.

> It is salutary to think that Wing-Commander Wallis in an autogyro which he has designed and built himself has a top speed of 120 m.p.h. and although weighing only half a ton would have kept up with the airliner all the way.
>
> Also in 1929, a Junkers aircraft with a specially adapted Bristol jupiter engine, flew to a new altitude record of nearly 8 miles. Again Wing-Commander Wallis is not to be outdone. He has ascended to over 3½ miles in his tiny aircraft, an aircraft in marked contrast to the all-metal Dornier flying ship which made its maiden flight in 1929. It was powered by twelve engines, had a crew of ten, carried 100 passengers and weighed 51 tons.

But the Wallis path has not been roses all the way …

In 1976 his lightest machine, weighing only 240 lb, crashed on take-off at Ken's Norfolk HQ, and was a total write-off. Ken was taken to hospital with a compound fracture of the ankle and his son David, who was his passenger, suffered cuts and bruises – although to put the matter in perspective it is the only time a Wallis machine has crashed.

And in setting his latest altitude record his oxygen equipment froze and for a time it was touch-and-go whether the veteran flier would survive.

Finance as always with pioneers is a constant problem and Ken has had to put his machine to all manner of purposes including government contracts, aerial surveying and photography – and film-making.

He has often been called in by the police. He searched and photographed areas of Surrey when the police were checking reports that six victims of Irish extremists had been buried in the locality.

When Lord 'Lucky' Lucan was hunted after his children's nanny was found murdered, there scurrying over the South Downs was Ken Wallis in one of his autogyros. Again the Devon police sought his assistance when a woman disappeared from the town of Salcombe with her son and daughter, aged seven and six respectively.

These real-life adventures were tame stuff to a man who, doubling for Sean Connery as James Bond, did all the flying sequences in the 007 film, *You Only Live Twice*. To double for Connery, Ken had to wear an open-necked sleeveless shirt and a helmet fitted with a dummy cine and TV camera. The scenes were shot over the volcanoes and rocky East China Sea coastline of Southern Japan. Flying above a 6,000-ft volcano at 6.30 in the morning the cold was intense and an open shirt gave little protection. To make matters worse, the helmet with the dummy camera on top was 'aerodynamically unstable' and greatly affected by the force of gravity – literally a headache for the pilot.

Connery being clean-shaven, Ken also had to remove his moustache which, he says, has 'never been the same since'.

The autogyro used was XR 943, dubbed *Little Nellie*, which had started life as a military aircraft. It carried working flame and smoke generators on the tail, 14 rockets in packs of 7, 50 parachute mines and 2 large guided missiles. Additionally there were 2 machine-guns, firing blanks for film effects. All of these devices were actually fired or launched during the film sequences.

Little Nellie also carried two-way radio and, in some of the sequences, a large Panavision camera, so big that it made it more of a camera carrying an autogyro rather than the other way round.

Despite this handicap, the Wallis autogyro successfully shot out of the sky four helicopters belonging to the villainous Spectre organization.

For an Italian-made film *Nick Carter*, Ken had to fly over the Amazon and the Brazilian jungle. 'The producer was so impressed that he made me fly under every river and railway bridge he could find.'

All of these are just exhilarating and, hopefully, profitable sidelines to a man dedicated to autogyro research and development, a man who describes himself as someone who has lifted himself higher – *with less* – than ever before. A point he amply proved when he won the Segrave Trophy for the first time. He simply closed up the rotor wings and wheeled his autogyro along Pall Mall to the Royal Automobile Club and through the front door – to the bewilderment of London's motorists and taxi-drivers.

His friend, Squadron-Leader John Crampton, who has himself flown more types of aircraft than the vast majority of pilots and is now himself a member of the Segrave Trophy Committee, representing the RAC, recalls his first meeting with Ken at RAF Scampton in 1950 when Ken was the station's armament officer.

> I remember being immensely impressed by his artistry in metal. He could make anything. And if he could not find a suitable tool for a job then he would make the tool, too.
>
> He was dreaming of an ultra-light rotary-wing personalized flying machine even then. He had it in mind to build something you could strap to yourself with a tiny engine driving contra-rotating rotors above your head. It was to be called the *Wallis Wearoplane* (ouch!). From Scampton he was seconded to the USAF Strategic Air Command at Offnutt Air Force Base, Omaha, and it was while he was in America that he took a long look at the Benson autogyro and decided to develop something better.

Which, of course, he did.

Benson took another road. In 1955, Dr Igor B. Benson designed a very simple open-seat Gyro-copter which he subsequently sold in kitform.

So what of the future of the Wallis autogyro?

It could revolutionize private flying since it is unlikely to cost more than the average car. Ken built most of his fleet of around two dozen for under £2,000 each and they are economical to run, consuming about three gallons in an hour's flying at 65 m.p.h.

For military and practical purposes they have already proven their worth and Ken has even landed them on cargo vessels in the stormy North Sea.

When military airfields are damaged by enemy bombers

the urgent task is to get them cleaned up enough for friendly aircraft to land. Before this can be done it is essential that the extent of the damage is known and that any unexploded bombs and/or booby traps are identified. This is where a Wallis autogyro, equipped with infra-red scanners, radio ground link and video and photographic systems comes in.

It is the ideal aircraft for the job and, apart from anything else, does not need another airfield from which to take off. It can operate in all weathers, day or night.

In addition to airfield damage reconnaissance, the Wallis has been employed in the detection of illicit graves, leaks in deep pipelines, crop disease, marine pollution, coastal and terrestrial ecology and archaeology.

'No other heavier-than-air craft approaches the power-to-weight ratio of the autogyro or its weight-lifting ability,' writes Neil Harrison, of *Flight Magazine*. 'Wherever it would help to have a man in the sky – with a camera, a radio transmitter, weapons or simply to observe – the autogyro offers perhaps the cheapest and the best all-round solution.'

Six more world records fell to Wing-Commander Wallis in 1988 and he was again nominated for the Segrave Trophy, being edged out by Martin Brundle. There was consolation for Ken, however, when the Duke of York, President of the Royal Aero Club, presented him with the Salemon Trophy 'for an outstanding performance by a British subject in a flying apparatus or device substantially designed or constructed in the United Kingdom'.

Let us leave the last word to John Crampton: 'Ken is a great man of our time. No one can write a history book about him yet. He's still busy making history.'

10 *'The CO is in the Drink'*

On only one occasion has the Segrave Trophy been awarded without a full meeting of the committee and this is how it happened.

On 2 April 1982 Argentine forces invaded the Falkland Islands and took control. Next day, the Security Council voted in favour of Argentine's withdrawal, to which the Argentine reaction was seizure of South Georgia, a dependency of the Falklands. On 5 April a British Task Force sailed from Portsmouth and so began one of the most complicated, highly technical and logistically difficult military operations in history.

On 25 April Royal Marines landed on South Georgia from helicopters and recaptured the territory without casualties. During the next few weeks the struggle became concentrated on the British Navy versus the Argentine Air Force. A British submarine torpedoed the enemy cruiser, *Belgrano*, 800 of the 1,042 crew surviving. The British *Sheffield*, frigates *Ardent* and *Antelope*, destroyer *Coventry* and Cunard container ship, *Atlantic Conveyor*, were all severely damaged or sunk with the loss of 82 lives.

All the time, British plans were leading to a counter-invasion and recapture of the Falklands and on 28 May 600 British paras captured Goose Green and Port Darwin on East Falkland.

The land battle was to last little more than a fortnight and on 15 June 1982, Major-General Jeremy Moore, commanding British land forces, accepted the surrender of the Argentine forces, led by Major-General Menendez.

Two days later 'the villain of the piece', General Leopoldo

Galtieri, was ousted as President of Argentine.

With the successful completion of this campaign against naked Hitler-type aggression, I telephoned Lord Camden and suggested to him that the efforts of the Task Force complied with all the requirements of the Segrave Trophy award. Courage in abundance, skill and initiative too. And, of course, a tremendous demonstration of the possibilities of transport by land, air and water. Brecky enthusiastically agreed. He also agreed that the award should be made as quickly as possible. So, instead of calling a committee meeting, I telephoned every member of the committee and asked for their agreement. Not one dissented – the Segrave Committee obviously had fewer 'wets' than the House of Commons. We all felt that the award was recognition of the bravery of men and women showing the spirit which had put the great in Great Britain.

After discussions in government circles it was agreed that the trophy be presented to Rear Admiral J. F. 'Sandy' Woodward, Commander of the Task Force, with Segrave Medals going to Major-General J. H. Moore, commander of the land forces; Wing-Commander A. M. Bowman, in charge of the air refuelling operation, of which more later; and Lt Col. D. R. Chaundler, of the Parachute Regiment. Thus all branches of the services engaged in the Falklands War, since war it was, were recognized.

The changing face of naval operations was well illustrated in the person of 'Sandy' Woodward, who is basically a submarine man. In the days of the great battleships, no submarine commander would have been put in command of an operation such as that confronting the Falklands Task Force but the nuclear submarine has become the most potent striking force any Navy can have and its importance was recognized in Admiral Woodward's appointment.

Fifty years old at the time – his birthday occurred in the middle of the war – he had originally graduated from Dartmouth and first went to sea as a midshipman on a submarine depot ship. Later he served on destroyers and cruisers before becoming a submarine specialist in 1954. His first command was HMS *Grampus* in 1961 and he was promoted to lieutenant-commander in 1962. Other sea commands alternated with postings ashore until he was appointed Captain Submarine Sea Training. In 1976 he assumed command of the guided missile destroyer HMS *Sheffield*, which was to figure prominently in the Falklands, and in 1978 returned to the Ministry of Defence as the Director of Naval Plans. He was promoted to rear admiral and assumed the duties of Flag Officer First Flotilla in 1981.

Married with two children, this quiet, sturdy Cornishman looks as if he could never be rattled – just the sort of man to be in charge of an operation such as the Falklands campaign.

Away from the Navy his interests are mathematics, stamp collecting and antique furniture but he is also an action man, his favourite sports being skiing and sailing (what else?).

John Jeremy Moore, the man who received the Argentine surrender, had led a colourful life since joining the Royal Marines in 1947. For eighteen months he was a rifle troop subaltern fighting the terrorists in Malaya and during this period he was awarded the Military Cross. On returning to the United Kingdom, he became a housemaster at the Royal Marine School of Music of which he subsequently became commandant. He held other home-based appointments until the Cyprus emergency when he served as Adjutant of 45 Commando. On returning home he was an instructor at the Royal Military Academy at Sandhurst for three years but returned to the Far East in 1962. As a captain, in command of L Company, 42 Commando, he participated in operations to quell the rebellion in Brunei and was awarded a bar to his Military Cross. He campaigned in Borneo, did tours of duty in Northern Ireland (and received the OBE) and during his time in command of 3 Commando trained in Arctic survival techniques, winter warfare, and skiing.

On 8 August 1979 he was promoted to major general and appointed major general Royal Marines Commando Forces. He and his wife, Veryan, have two daughters and a son.

The Argentinians undoubtedly would have wished that John Jeremy Moore had continued his ardent interest in music by remaining commandant of the RM School of Music. They did not appreciate his more aggressive talents.

The airman who collected the second Segrave Medal was a unique exponent of the arts of skill and science in transport.

Wing-Commander A. M. Bowman commanded the Operation CORPORATE Victor K2 detachment at Ascension Island and the arrival of Victor tanker aircraft at Wideawake Airfield heralded the largest air-to-air refuelling task ever undertaken by the Royal Air Force.

The first problem Great Britain faced in defeating the Falklands invaders involved dealing with the great distances between home bases and the Islands. Ships faced a long voyage, aircraft needed refuelling.

Despite a British base at Ascension Island there were still 3,400 nautical miles to go to the Falklands and this distance dictated that air refuelling was a prerequisite for all air operations over the South Atlantic. Throughout hostilities, Vulcan, Nimrod and Hercules aircraft, not to mention the Victor tankers themselves, flew missions of unprecedented length. The air-refuelling support of these missions required large formations of tanker aircraft, very complex refuelling plans and the pioneering of new operational concepts.

The RAF said that Wing-Commander Bowman

> excelled in the unique challenge of the situation. His inventiveness, enthusiasm and tireless energy were keyed to resolving the many demands made upon the detachment's resources. During his time at Ascension Island, Wing Commander Bowman flew more than 230 hours on refuelling operations and thus his spirited leadership was as significant in the air as on the ground.
>
> The brilliant success of the long-range air-refuelling missions in support of forces in the South Atlantic was due in no small measure to Wing Commander Bowman's exceptional endeavours.
>
> In his vital contribution to Operation CORPORATE, Wing Commander Bowman so furthered the potential and the flexibility of modern air power that he is a most worthy nomination for the Segrave Medal to be awarded to the Royal Air Force.

Home base for Wing-Commander Bowman, his wife and three daughters was RAF Marham, Norfolk.

It is doubtful if any serviceman has ever arrived at a posting in the manner of the third recipient of the Segrave Medal in 1982. Over hundreds of years of warfare many a squaddy must have expressed a desire to see his commanding officer 'in the drink' or some other variation of the fertilizer business.

In the case of Lt Col D. R. Chaundler of the Paras, it happened – literally.

He was sitting quietly at a desk in the Ministry of Defence when word came through of the death in the Falklands of Lt Col H. Jones, OBE. His successor as CO of 2 Battalion, the Parachute Regiment was to be Colonel Chaundler.

He was flown down to the South Atlantic by Hercules and parachuted from 800 feet into the freezing sea where he was picked up by a frigate and transported by ship and helicopter to join his battalion at Goose Green.

Epilogue: Last Lament

The pipe-major of the Scots Guards turned on his heel and the skirl of his pipes swelled to fill the chapel with sound as he strode towards the door with measured pace.

He turned into the street and marched slowly towards Wellington Barracks. In the chapel no one stirred or said a word until the sound of the pipes faded away and there was silence.

Thus his comrades and colleagues, family and friends said goodbye to the Marquess Camden.

The Bishop of Rochester officiated at the memorial service, assisted by the chaplain to the Household Division, the Guards. Readings were given by the new Marquess Camden, 'a chip off the old block'; his son, now the Earl of Brecknock; and an old friend, Colonel Raymond Lees.

Apart from Rosemary, Lady Camden, and other members of the family, the congregation included a large slice of *Debrett*, *Burke's Peerage* and *Who's Who*, in addition to more humble mortals.

Motor sport was represented by the Duke of Richmond and Gordon who, as Freddie March, was a leading Brooklands driver of the 1930s; Earl Howe; former British saloon car champion and rally driver, Jack Sears; J. P. Broadley of the Aston Martin Owners Club; Derek Guy of Castrol; and Ken Shierson of the Auto-Cycle Union, of which the Marquess Camden had been president.

Jeffrey Rose, chairman of the RAC, was there as was his predecessor, rugby international Sir Carl Aarvold. The AA was represented by its director-general and the Guards Club by its president. The Royal National Lifeboat Institution was represented. So was the Royal Yacht Squadron. Lord Montagu of the National Motor Museum was there. And the commanding officer of the Scots Guards and his adjutant.

The congregation reflected the many activities and interests of the Marquess Camden – Brecky, as he was known to his friends from his days as Viscount Brecknock.

He had been Henry Segrave's friend and confidant and he had been his team manager on many a record attempt. More than any other he had helped to keep Segrave's memory alive, not least through the years he had served on the Segrave Committee, many of them as chairman.

The loyalty he gave to Segrave he gave to many others he called his friends. Which is why that sunny morning the Guards Chapel was full to overflowing.

An aristocrat to his fingertips, he yet drew his friends from all parts of society. It mattered not to him what a man did for a living or who his parents had been – if he was a decent chap then that was all right for Brecky. Duke or dustman, it made no odds.

Gus Kuhn, the famous early speedway rider, was one of Brecky's pals. Gus apparently used to deliver meat to the Camden residence and would tarry a while to pass on tips on how to broadside a motor-bike on cinders. Brecky retained an interest in speedway racing until he died and was always ready to talk about 'dear old Gus'. Another old friend he could recount some tales about was Flight-Lieutenant Staniforth, of Schneider Trophy seaplane race fame.

Brecky's interests were so widespread that wherever he went he would meet friends. Military service with the Scots Guards; Gold Staff at the Coronation of King George VI; a member of the Cavalry, Guards, Pratts (the family name, incidentally), Turf and RAC (of which he was at one time senior vice-chairman) Clubs; chairman, patron or trustee of many local organizations and charities in his home county of Kent; these are perhaps what one would expect of a senior peer of the realm.

Yet his entry in *Who's Who* revealed other facets of the man. He gave his recreations as shooting, boxing, motor-racing, yachting and motor-boat racing. Shooting again appears in many people's entries but not, perhaps, boxing.

Brecky's interest was such that at one time he was a director of the National Sporting Club where many bouts were staged and in his younger days he boxed for the Army.

As Viscount Brecknock he raced and rallied, worked for Sunbeams and helped Segrave. Later he served in various capacities for the RAC Motor Sports Council, the British Automobile Racing Club and the Aston Martin Owners Club, which was a particular favourite of his. He was Vice-Commodore of the Royal Yacht Squadron and Rear-Admiral of the Royal Motor Yacht Club so you always knew where to find him during Cowes.

He was also a keen worker for road safety and an officer of the Company of Veteran Motorists.

His association with Segrave began when they were at Eton and continued when both joined the Sunbeam Company (Brecky became a director of the associated Darracq and Bayard companies) and when De Hane went into action, Brecky was there to help in any way possible.

He was with him on that epic expedition to USA in 1929 with the *Golden Arrow*. Bill Rootes, who would accompany the party to the States, threw a 'send-off' celebration in the Rootes' car showrooms in Piccadilly where the *Golden Arrow* and *Miss England* were on display, and just about anyone who was anyone attended.

There was the Prince of Wales, the Prime Minister Stanley Baldwin, the Home Secretary Joynson Hicks, the American Ambassador and many more besides. Gilbert Frankau, the novelist, was also there and many years afterwards Brecky drew my attention to an account the writer gave of that occasion in his book *Self-Portrait*.

Apparently De Hane and Frankau were introduced and Frankau, gazing at the *Golden Arrow*, commented, 'I wouldn't drive that car for all the money in the world.'

Prophetically De Hane replied, 'It's this boat that puts the breeze up me. Kill me before I'm through with her, I expect.'

A few days later, the Segraves, Brecky, Captain Irving and the rest of the team were in Daytona and such gloomy thoughts were forgotten.

Only Frankau remembered ...

For an action man – he raced at Brooklands and rallied

between the wars in addition to his yachting, shooting and boxing – and a man of considerable education – Ludgrove, Eton and Sandhurst – Lord Camden was surprisingly nervous when it came to public speaking.

Even at the last moment he would be dropping suggestions that perhaps someone else might make the speech and I really believe it was purgatory for him. There was one occasion when he was making the presentations at the finish of the RAC Rally in Harrogate. I introduced him and handed over the mike. Then to my astonishment his voice alternately boomed then died away to a whisper, boomed and died away.

Then it dawned on me. The hand-mike had an on–off switch and in his nervousness Brecky was flicking it on and off with his thumb.

His other weakness was absent-mindedness. At the conclusion of another rally, this time at London Airport's Excelsior Hotel, he came rushing up to me and said, 'Phil, my car has been taken. What shall I do?' At that moment rally-driver John Gott, who in business life was a chief constable, hove into view.

'There's John,' I pointed out. 'He'll know what to do.'

The 'stolen' car number and description were circulated to all police forces and the great hunt began. Two days later the car was found. The Excelsior had a front entrance and a similar-looking back entrance. Brecky had been looking for his car at the front while all the time it had been at the back!

However, when it came to choosing a winner of the Segrave Trophy, no one could be more thorough than Lord Camden. He was determined to be fair and often when the rest of the committee seemed to have more or less made up their mind the chairman would refer back to another candidate and say, 'Let's make sure we've considered all the factors in this case.' Quite rightly, he was adamant that any winner of a trophy bearing the name of his closest friend should be worthy of it.

So it was that in 1980 when Lady Arran was presented with the trophy and her crew with Segrave Medals there was an additional presentation – a Segrave Medal was presented to the Marquess Camden in recognition of fifty years' active association with the Segrave Trophy.

He was taken completely by surprise and quite overcome,

but if ever a man earned a Segrave Medal he did.

Four years later he was dead but his work continues, with Ford's chief executive Derek Barron chairing the awarding committee meetings with the thoroughness that marked the Camden regime and, at the annual presentation, we are always delighted to greet Brecky's widow, Rosemary.

In one of the last letters he wrote to me he said, 'I am delighted that you will still be in the offing and will continue as Secretary of the Segrave Trophy Award.'

All present and correct, m'lud.

Past Winners of the Segrave Trophy

1930	Air Commodore Sir Charles Kingsford-Smith
1931	Squadron-Leader Bert Hinkler
1932	Amy Johnson
1933	Captain Sir Malcolm Campbell
1934	Ken Waller
1935	Captain G. E. T. Eyston
1936	Jean Batten
1937	Flying-Officer A. E. Clouston
1938	Major A. T. Goldie Gardner
1939	Captain Sir Malcolm Campbell
1946	Geoffrey Raoul de Havilland (posthumous)
1947	John Rhodes Cobb
1948	John Douglas Derry
1951	Geoffrey Duke
1953	Squadron-Leader Neville Duke
1955	Donald Campbell
1956	Peter Twiss
1957	Stirling Moss
1958	Donald Campbell
1960	Tom Brooke-Smith
1962	A. W. Bedford
1964	Donald Campbell
1966	Donald Campbell (posthumous)
1968	Wing-Commander Ken Wallis
1969	Bruce McLaren
1970	Brian Trubshaw
1973	Jackie Stewart
1974	Major John Blashford-Snell

1975	Roger Clark, coupled with the names of Jim Porter, Stuart Turner and the Ford Motor Company
1976	Peter Collins
1977	Barry Sheene
1978	Group-Captain John Cunningham
1979	Mike Hailwood
1980	Lady Arran
1982	Rear-Admiral Sandy Woodward and the men and women of the British Falklands Task Force
1983	Richard Noble
1984	Barry Sheene
1985	Wing-Commander Ken Wallis
1986	Richard Branson
1987	Eve Jackson
1988	Martin Brundle
1989	Bob and Joe Ives

The award was suspended during the Second World War, 1940–45 and in other years where the trophy has not been awarded it has been because, in the opinion of the committee, there has been no achievement of sufficient merit to earn the award.

Appendix: Segrave Awards 1989

A record number of thirteen nominations was received for the 1989 Segrave Trophy and at their meeting on Thursday, 22 February 1990, the awarding committee narrowed this down to a shortlist of four.

A final vote gave the verdict to Hampshire farmers Bob and Joe Ives for winning the tenth Camel Trophy against competitors from thirteen countries. The event was held in the Brazilian Amazon and each team had to negotiate 1,300 km and nine special tasks in identical Land Rover One Diesel Turbos. It was a fight against the elements, the jungle and waist-deep mud, and the British pair fought off strong challenges from the Spaniards, the Turks and the Brazilians in turn.

The other nominees to be involved in the final voting were Steve Webster and Tony Hewitt, World Sidecar champions for the third year in succession.

For the first time in the history of the trophy, the awarding committee also decided to make a special commendation. Stuart Bladon, a motoring writer, broke the world fuel economy record for production vehicles with a figure of 112.01 miles per gallon. Chairman Derek Barron said, 'Green issues are rightly of much concern today and Stuart Bladon's effort, worthy of nomination for the trophy, makes a significant contribution towards matters of ecology.'

Bibliography

Blashford-Snell, John, *In the Steps of Stanley* (Hutchinson, 1975)

Boddy, William, *The Story of Brooklands*, three vols (Grenville Publishing, 1948/9/50)

———, *Montlhery*, Montagu Motor Books (Cassell, 1961)

Campbell, Lady Dorothy, *Malcolm Campbell* (Hutchinson, 1951)

Clark, Roger with Robson, Graham, *Sideways ... to Victory* (Motor Racing Publications, 1976)

Clew, Jeff, *Lucky All My Life* (Haynes–G.T. Foulis, 1979)

Drackett, Phil, *Motor Racing* (Foyles Handbooks, 1952)

———, *Like Father, Like Son* (Clifton Books, 1969)

———, *Rally of the Forests* (Pelham Books, 1970)

———, *Motor Racing Champions* (Purnell, 1974)

———, *The RAC Rally* (Haynes–G.T. Foulis, 1980)

Eyston, Capt. G.E.T., *Fastest on Earth* (Floyd Clymer)

Foxworth, Thomas G., *The Speed Seekers* (Macdonald and James, 1975)

Gavin, Jim, *The Ford Escort and Rally Sport* (Pelham Books, 1973)

Knowles, Arthur and Campbell, Lady Dorothy, *Donald Campbell, CBE* (George Allen & Unwin, 1969)

Macauley, Ted, *Mike the Bike – Again* (Cassell, 1980)

McComb, F. Wilson, *The Story of the MG Sportscar* (J.M. Dent, 1972)

Posthumus, Cyril, *Sir Henry Segrave* (Batsford, 1961)

Raymond, Robert, *Stirling Moss* (Motor Racing Publications, 1953)

Sheene, Barry with Beacham, Ian, *Barry Sheene: The Story So Far* (W.H. Allen, 1976)

Stewart, Jackie with Dymock, Eric, *World Champion* (Pelham Books, 1970)

Tours, Hugh, *Parry Thomas, Designer-driver* (Batsford, 1959)

Index